BETWEEN A ROCK
AND A HARD PLACE

BETWEEN
A ROCK

AND A HARD PLACE

MARK HATFIELD

WORD BOOKS, PUBLISHER
WACO, TEXAS

First Printing, April 1976
Second Printing, July 1976
Third Printing, July 1976
Fourth Printing, April 1977

BETWEEN A ROCK AND A HARD PLACE
Copyright © 1976 by Word, Incorporated, Waco, Texas

Scripture quotations except those otherwise marked are
from *The New English Bible,* copyright © The Delegates of
The Oxford University Press and The Syndics of the Cambridge
University Press, 1961, 1970, and are used by permission.

Scripture quotations marked RSV are from the Revised Standard
Version of the Bible, copyright 1946 (renewed 1973), 1956
and © 1971 by the Division of Christian Education of the
National Council of the Churches of Christ in the United States
of America, and are used by permission.

Grateful acknowledgment is made for the use of the article
"Nixon Hears War Called a 'Sin'" by James T. Wooten, which
appeared in the *New York Times* February 2, 1973. Copyright
© 1973 by the New York Times Company. Reprinted by permission.

ISBN #0-87680-427-X
Library of Congress catalog card number: 75-42906
Printed in the United States of America

Dedicated to Elizabeth, Mark, Jr., Theresa, and Charles Vincent (Visko), who have been both inspiration and challenge in keeping their parents dependent on the continuing Grace of Christ.

Contents

Preface

When I finally grasped the relational dimension to the faith, how much more I realized my dependence upon others. The open sharing with people has no limitation in the opportunity to refine and redefine one's own journey of faith.

How difficult it would be to list all who have contributed to the evolution of my thinking and understanding concerning the issues and material incorporated in this book: the constancy of Antoinette's love; the edification of the Reverend Richard C. Halverson's Sunday sermons; the writings of many persons; the aid of Jack Robertson, Keith Kennedy, and Lon Fendall; and the sublime fellowship with other believers, to name but a few.

In some areas of a person's thinking one finds the compatibility of an alter ego. Wes Michaelson, with whom I have been associated for over seven years, has been such a person to me. Hour upon hour of brainstorming, research, and phrasing together have resulted in a truly joint endeavor which we gladly share with all who would read.

Chapter 1

Politics
and Pretension

I T WAS a hot and muggy day in Washington—the kind that makes you understand why many visiting ambassadors used to get hardship pay because of the bad climate. "I'm glad to be getting out of this place," I told the trusted friend who picked me up at the office. We were on our way to National Airport, where I would take a flight back to Oregon to join my wife and children for what was left of this summer of 1971.

But it was not just the joy of seeing them nor the prospect of escaping the oppressive heat which made me anxious to get on the plane. I was fed up with the entire climate of the capital—all the pompous pretension, the dehumanizing relationships, the prestige-seeking social life, and the seeming impotence, frustration, and emptiness of political endeavor.

Usually I held thoughts like these well within me. But now they kept surfacing to set the tone of our conversation.

I thought about the year before. The country had been nearly torn apart by the policies of President Richard Nixon in Southeast Asia. The day preceding the Cambodian invasion, Senator George McGovern and I, not knowing what might lie ahead, introduced an amendment to cut off all funds for the War. Suddenly we found ourselves thrust into the middle of a furious national and Congressional debate which raged throughout the summer of 1970. By the fall, it culminated in a Senate vote on the McGovern-Hatfield Amendment, which we lost 55–42.

Then it began to appear that I was losing in Oregon as well. Those close to me said my political base was eroding. I knew to a degree this could be true. The "establishment" and the "loyal" Republicans were becoming increasingly infuriated at my pattern of votes against the Nixon Administration. In particular, they disliked my association with Senator McGovern. It seemed that whatever President Nixon favored, I opposed—the ABM, the SST, the War, Haynsworth, Carswell, and so on. The President fueled the fires by sending Vice-President Agnew around the country calling all of us with similar views "radic-libs." Then the Administration staged a public campaign against Republican Senator Charles Goodell, who was running for re-election in New York. His defeat was seen by other Republicans who were differing with Mr. Nixon as an obvious threat against them. My voting record, just as nonsupportive of the Nixon Administration as Goodell's, gave ominous warning that his fate in 1970 could also be mine in 1972. Meanwhile, the War went on.

By the spring of 1971 we had taken our case to the Senate once again, getting two more votes in our favor, but still losing. However, another amendment with nearly identical language, offered by two Republican Senators who had previously been in support of the War, received 49 votes. It would have received 50, enough to pass, had not Senator John Stennis persuaded the late Senator B. Everett Jordan at the last minute to change his vote and oppose the amendment.

As we neared the airport, my friend pointed out that half the Senate was actually on record against continuing funds for the War in Vietnam. Yet they had never all voted that way at the same time, so the War went on unimpeded, in disregard of clear Constitutional principles. I had all but given up any practical hope that Congress could effectively alter the course of President Nixon's Vietnam policies.

It seemed so futile to me. Back in Oregon, the State Chairman of Oregon's Republican Party had publicly invited me to leave the Party and become a Democrat. Polls showed that I could be beaten both in a Republican primary race and by a Democratic opponent. To get re-elected in 1972 would be a struggle, but that really wasn't the point. I had always faced tough political adversaries, both in primary and general elections. And the opposition had increased notably since the keynote address to the Republican National Convention in 1964, when I first publicly spoke against the War; and especially since 1965 and 1966, when I voted at the National Governors' Conferences against President Johnson's war policies.

This was not the first time, then, people had said my actions were alienating the voters. And frankly, I didn't really care that much. I had heard these warnings before, thought through the implications, and decided that the issues transcended any importance on my political career.

Then something far more distressing than that began to happen. Fellow evangelical Christians began writing and telling me how much they hated my position and, more than that, doubted the sincerity of my faith. At the Conservative Baptist Men's retreat the previous fall (in my own home denomination) there was talk of a walkout when I stood up to give an address. I had spoken annually at their retreat in Oregon, and I intended to talk to them that year about the meaning of Christian fellowship. But many expressed doubt that I was qualified to be included in that fellowship because of the political positions I had taken on issues such as the War. Letters, visits and other encounters conveyed the same message.

I was shocked, dismayed, depressed. Down inside of me

my feelings began to eat away in a manner I could barely control. Part of me wanted to lash back. To this day I cannot understand how believing Christians who have given their allegiance to the Prince of Peace could cheer on the nation in that despicable and inhumane War. Yet, I knew that I had no more right to judge the validity of their personal faith than they had to judge mine.

What am I doing all this for anyway? I asked myself. What's the purpose of coming back to Washington, living this kind of life, splitting up time between the demands of being a Senator and the responsibilities of being a husband to my wife and father to my four children? Of course, I would remind myself, there are all these issues I feel are so vital to our nation's future. Yet, it seemed nearly impossible to change them through anything I could do as a United States Senator. Going out and giving stirring speeches about the immorality of the War, I would sense a tremendous responsiveness; but then, I'd go home, and the audience would go home, and the War would go on. Nothing would really seem to be different. It was the same with the whole assault other Senators and I made trying to cut just two or three billion from the money requested by the Pentagon. There was merit in raising crucial issues, but the battles were never won. It seemed, moreover, that they never could be won.

It didn't really help that often people would tell me how much hope in the system my actions in the Senate gave them. Rather, that always made me feel strange, for it seemed that they had more hope than I. And I couldn't share my deepest thoughts about the ineptitude of the Congress or the resistance of our political system to fundamental change.

We had reached the airport when my companion articulated my own question for me, wondering out loud whether it was all really worth it. (He had no idea that, just a few months before, I had considered resigning from office. It would have been an easy way out, but probably an irresponsible one, breaking the trust put in me by the people of Oregon in 1966.) We walked quietly to the terminal door. Finally I turned and said to my young friend, "I know this

much. If I had to make the decision today, I wouldn't run
again for the Senate."

A politician can voice such thoughts openly with very few
people. In our culture we have bred such an idolatry of
power that everyone assumes its apparent possession brings
unquestioned fulfillment.

During that summer and fall, reporters frequently asked
me about my prospects for re-election. I discussed the situation as I saw it, but always said clearly I had not decided
whether I would seek re-election to the Senate. The reaction
was revealing. No one ever believed me.

Newspaper editors and political observers speculated about
my comments. Just a political ploy, they said, to help create
a good image. Eventually, when the time was right, I would
announce my intention to run again for the Senate. After
all, a United States Senator has achieved significant power;
naturally he would never give that up voluntarily.

Any honest politician would have to admit to the ambition
and ego that motivate his or her journey in public life. (I
ran for the state legislature not because I wanted to spend
my life as a member of Oregon's House of Representatives,
but because I thought I could become a State Senator, and
then perhaps Secretary of State, and maybe even Governor.)
There are always persuasive rationalizations, of course, to
discount that motive: You are there to serve your constituents. Or, you have a commitment to certain causes and ideals
—to fight for justice, make America more humane, save the
world, or whatever. How rare, though, to see a politician
truly jeopardize his or her political career because of a commitment to principle. Compromises, the politician explains,
are required for gaining greater power and a better opportunity for achieving one's ideals. In that process, however,
the means seem to become the end. One's efforts and energies
are eventually dominated by the need for self-maintenance.

Richard Nixon, at the pinnacle of power, chose to protect
his ego and position rather than to defend the Constitution
of the United States. But how different were his pride and
ambition from that of most other politicians? Watergate,

commonly assumed to be the result of one individual's personal corruption, in actuality went far deeper, revealing the corrupting lust for power that characterizes our entire political system. Countless individuals in public life today, if confronted with the same situation as Richard Nixon, would have acted very much as he did.

The allurement of power and honor subtly but malignantly grows within the politician, often gaining control of one's whole being before it is discovered.

An important, but often ignored, factor is the essentially dehumanizing character of relationships in the political world. People relate to a Senator's prestige, title, and influence. They assume that his opinions must automatically be more accurate than their own. A Senator grows accustomed to being treated in this reverential way. Within, this can breed the belief that he is more important, more virtuous, and wiser than the average citizens whom he represents.

Frequently such reverence reaches absurd degrees. Once, I had flown to a nearby city to deliver an address at the university. As usual, the special delegation which greeted me had arranged for various meetings and a press conference from the moment I walked off the plane. There was not a moment to relax. In the midst of this flurry of hand-shaking and question-answering, I became vividly aware of one elementary human necessity: I needed to spend about sixty seconds in the nearest men's room. Of course, that wasn't on the schedule. I was hustled into the waiting car and we sped toward the auditorium. When I finally made known to my escorts the urgency of my need, they were filled with consternation. The thought of simply pulling into the first grimy service station—which by that time would have been a heaven-sent answer to my prayers—seemed totally incongruous to them. After all, I was a Senator, and Senators somehow were different from normal people. Convincing them I was no respecter of bathrooms and not the least bit embarrassed to ask a service station manager for the key to his men's room took all my persuasive powers.

Another little-recognized hazard of senatorial life is the deferential air that continually surrounds him. For instance, my staff of about thirty-five committed people may hold some disagreements on policies adopted, but in the end they always are there to bolster me, assuring me of the rightness of my decisions, and encouraging me in what I do. As a result I always have a faithful group who will support my ego.

While my staff probes me to consider all aspects of a difficult decision, constituents and others who visit me in Washington, D.C., are frequently overcome by an unqualified sense of awe which inhibits any real dialogue. They treat me with so much more honor than honesty that strong disagreements with my positions rarely get expressed. When they do, it is with almost an apologetic air. Of course, there are notable exceptions. For the most part, however, people mainly evidence the honor they feel at being in the presence of a United States Senator; the danger is that I can begin to feel worthy of all that praise.

My every move through the Senate perpetuates this ego massage. When I leave my office to go to the Senate floor, an elevator comes immediately at senatorial command, reversing its direction if necessary and bypassing the floors of the other bewildered passengers aboard in order to get me to the basement. As I walk down the corridor, a policeman notices me coming and rings for a subway car to wait for my arrival and take me to the Capitol Building. The elevator operator, the Capitol policeman, and the subway drivers all deferentially greet me. On the subway car I may take the front seat, which is reserved for Senators who may ride there alone; tourists already seated there are removed by a policeman unless I insist otherwise. At the Capitol another elevator marked FOR SENATORS ONLY takes me to the Senate floor. There at the raising of an eyebrow a page comes to give me a glass of water, deliver a message, or get whatever I need. Aides scurry about telling me when votes will occur on which bills, although no one bothers me with all the details unless I ask.

Senators greet each other on a cordial, first-name basis, trying to be dignified, statesmenlike gentlemen. On the Senate floor we address one another as "the distinguished

Senator from North Carolina" and usually add "and my long and good friend." This custom does maintain a certain orderliness and decorum in the legislative process, preventing political differences from erupting into personal attacks. On the whole, however, such protocol creates a façade of artificial cordiality, cloaking true feelings and inhibiting close relationships.

Rarely are there any intimate personal friends within the U.S. Senate. Relationships remain at a formal, restrained level with only a few exceptions, such as bonds of friendship that can develop out of the Wednesday morning Senate prayer breakfast groups. At those times we may discard our "masks" and transcend the impersonal barriers normally isolating us. But this always goes against the established pattern. For the most part, Senators seldom relate to their peers or their constituents in simple human terms. It becomes an almost unconscious reaction to relate as a "Senator" to others, for that is how they relate to us.

No profession except perhaps the Metropolitan Opera nurtures the prima donna complex as does successful political life, and I have not been immune to all these pressures and forces. But by that hot summer in 1971, after nearly a quarter century of political life, I had developed some real detachment from all the psychological enticements that come with the aura of power. And whenever political life is stripped of all its honorific pretensions and ego gratifications, then its real meaning comes into fundamental question.

It is embarrassing to acknowledge how little actual power rests in the hands of most individual Senators and Representatives. Since World War II, the influence and power of the Executive Branch has totally overwhelmed the Congress in determining the course of national policies. What real power Congress does have is vested largely in those few members who serve as Committee Chairmen. Reform efforts in the House of Representatives have barely changed this reality. The plain truth is that upper-level bureaucrats in the Executive Branch, whose names are unknown to the American people, have far more actual influence over our nation's policies than the Senators whose faces are recognized in millions of households across America.

Charles Robinson, for instance, wields enormous power over U.S. international policy on food and energy. He is an assistant to Henry Kissinger. General Brent Scrowcraft, working in the White House as another Kissinger assistant, has wide influence over our policies of national security throughout the globe. Don Paarlberg has a substantial effect, as an assistant to Earl Butz, upon our agricultural economic policies. Such a list could continue with hundreds of names of those who, in actuality, run the government, exerting power and making choices of far deeper consequence than those typically left to the people elected to public office. Centralized political power in Washington has created an Executive government so impowered by its own momentum and self-justifying rationale of its duties that the points at which Congress influences or directs this massive bureaucracy are tenuous, intermittent, and frequently only marginal in overall effect. And in the past few years, Congress has made only timid and tentative efforts to reverse this trend.

What kind of influence does a member of Congress have then? Is there any concrete fashion in which he can use it? Primarily, it seems to be limited to obtaining certain projects or special considerations from the government for the home district or state. In my own case, for instance, as a member of the Interior Committee as well as the Public Works Subcommittee and Interior Subcommittee of the Appropriations Committee, I have been able to obtain the funding for certain projects of high importance to Oregon. Even here, this has come merely because I have obtained positions of sufficient seniority on the right committees.

Objectively, the whole process seems rather absurd. Why should the money appropriated by the Federal Government and the programs it adopts be influenced simply by which member of Congress, from what state, holds a particular position of influence on a Congressional committee? Yet that factor shapes, in very large measure, the limited influence Congress asserts over the workings of our government and the welfare of our nation. What real power a member of Congress may come to acquire is nearly always parochial; rarely is it national.

Most members of Congress try to pride themselves as being "influential." They portray the "successful" member of Congress as one who can manipulate the federal bureaucracy, with its hodgepodge of grants and programs, effectively enough to win various forms of largesse for the constituents. Small wonder that in building a record of what they achieve to benefit their constituents they attempt to take credit for any government project announced in their state or district whether they had any influence over it or not.

But the political system tends to force my colleagues and me to pay far more attention to how "effective" we look than to how "effective" we actually are. Most Senators, for instance, spend the vast majority of their time and staff resources on cosmetic efforts. Too often, far too little time is left to the hard work of legislation that is our primary responsibility. Needless to say, that is a far cry from what our founding fathers envisioned when they set up the legislative branch as that arm of government in which the power of the people to control the destiny of their nation would most firmly reside.

By that day in 1971 I was becoming more a part of this system. My evolving committee positions from one term of seniority were allowing me to exert guidance over certain appropriations and programs affecting Oregon. As I looked into the future, it was clear that such expanding influence could enable me to render increasingly valuable service for the interests of my state. Such considerations carried weight, for part of my Constitutional duty is to serve the needs of my constituency; that must never be neglected. Yet for me, this alone could not be the motive for seeking continued service in public life. I believe there is little ultimate meaning in trying to sell oneself to the people as a politician who can successfully manipulate the federal bureaucracy to their own benefit.

Political service must be rooted in a philosophy of society's overall well-being, with a broad vision of how the body

politic serves the people through its corporate structures.
The heart of one's service in the political order must be
molded by ideals, principles, and values that express how
we, in the words of the Constitution, are "To form a more
perfect union, establish justice, insure domestic tranquility,
provide for the common defense, promote the general welfare, and secure the blessings of liberty to ourselves and our
posterity." Political service must flow out of such a commitment. Convictions about war and peace, about the priorities
governing the expenditure of federal funds, about the patterns of economic wealth and distribution, about the stewardship of our nation's resources, about the government's
responsibility toward the oppressed and dispossessed both in
our land and throughout the world, about our nation's
system of law and justice, and about the meaning of human
liberty—these should be at the core of one's desire to seek
public office. They should be the basis upon which citizens
evaluate the abilities of another to serve them. Here is where
the true meaning of the political process is intended to rest.

How sad it is that political discourse and action so rarely
center on these concerns. It took the most massive scandal in
our nation's history and the devastating loss of faith in government by a majority of our citizens to temporarily awaken
the Congress to our purposes and values as a nation. Only
after countless and ruthless assaults on our Constitution
throughout the War and the Watergate scandal did Congress
belatedly face the task of trying to hold the system accountable to its ideals. The normalcy of politics postulates that
such ideals are, for all practical purposes, disregarded. At
best, they form stirring rhetoric for speeches to constituents.
Rarely are they what move men and women to seek and
preserve political power.

A façade of statesmanlike idealism conceals a brothel of
egomania and lust for power which prostitute those in political life for often nothing more than personal vainglory.

I was sick and tired of this all that day, five years ago,
and countless other days before and since then. As the plane
climbed out of Washington, I was relieved. I had little
desire to return.

Chapter 2

Power
As Servanthood

FAVORING colored oleo despite the impassioned opposition of dairy farmers in my district was hardly an historic profile in courage for a young state legislator. It began a pattern for me, however, which later led to the successful advocacy of a civil rights public accommodations law when many considered this an un-American heresy. The progressive steps during my career in state politics had threatened to place me in political jeopardy. Yet, I took them with pragmatic care and accompanied them with defensive tactics of reassurance to those potentially alienated.

Politically I was a success, never having lost an election. As a young moderate Governor in the 1960s, the national press said I was "Presidential timber."

Then the War came. My opposition was neither politically

calculated nor strategically planned. It came intuitively, emotionally, from my depths.

This reaction was molded by those days in 1945 when I had witnessed firsthand the anguished suffering of the Vietnamese; then I realized the total immorality of France's colonial imperialistic posture which the United States was still pursuing two decades later. The wanton desecration of life these policies produced revealed an utterly depraved inhumanity.

Fundamentally, the roots of my response were spiritual. As best I could I followed the beckoning to seek God's will. A unique inner abandonment flowed from heeding what my heart sensed to be truth; the consequences faded into irrelevancy.

What resulted seemed pragmatically senseless and politically disastrous. Such often is the way of faith. Naturally, I sought the love and encouragement of others whose allegiance belonged to the same Lord. That is why the spiritual rejection which emanated from many quarters of the evangelical community was so devastating. When my convictions alienated me from the Christian community I felt called to serve, I began to reconsider my calling to the political vocation.

Certain instances, though, gave me deep encouragement, demonstrating that some fellow evangelicals were understanding the implications of the Gospel in radically new ways. The first concrete evidence came in June of 1970, during the national convulsions following the invasion of Cambodia two months earlier.

Dave Hubbard had asked me to give the commencement address at Fuller Theological Seminary that spring, and I left for Pasadena, California, with mixed emotions. I was at a total loss to know how to relate to fellow theologically conservative Christians and was filled with considerable anxiety, not sure at all what to expect. Furthermore, as happened so frequently during those days, some of Fuller's conservative, wealthy supporters had made known to people at the seminary their displeasure over my appearance. Continually, it

seemed as though I was becoming a divisive force within the evangelical community, a role I had no desire to play. Yet, I felt compelled to say what was on my heart, without compromising my convictions. But I had no idea how my address would be received; in some ways I was expecting the worst.

The commencement ceremonies were being held at the First Methodist Church of Pasadena, close to the seminary campus. As I entered, immediately I sensed the warmth of this large audience. They welcomed me generously and enthusiastically in a way that caught me quite off guard. Then, just as I was about to begin my address, students in the balcony held up a sign which read "We're with you, Mark." It is difficult fully to describe all that went on within me. Somehow that one act symbolized so much that I had been longing to sense. There was an inner surge of joy, peace, and strength which I vividly recall to this day. These brothers and sisters were really with me; their acceptance created a sense of spiritual solidarity which I had rarely experienced from any segments within the Church.

When the students receiving degrees came forward I was stunned once again when almost two-thirds of them, I would guess, were wearing black arm bands in protest against the continuing war in Indochina. Again, this simple symbolic act coming from these students had a profound effect on my heart. It demonstrated to me that there were countless evangelicals, who because of their faith in Christ, could not condone the immoral and barbarian violence our nation was inflicting throughout Indochina.

While I was meeting with faculty and students after the commencement address a letter was handed to me. It was a petition stating that the undersigned fully supported me as a Christian brother in my effort to halt our involvement in Indochina, and specifically endorsed the McGovern-Hatfield Amendment to cut off funds for the War. It was signed by over half of the faculty of Fuller Seminary. Once again I was overwhelmed by the spirit of love and acceptance from the Fuller community. One of the most significant events of that entire year, this came as an initial sign of hope about the po-

tential response among evangelical Christians to the issues
of social and political concern which I felt were critical to
our witness.

The publication of the *Post-American* in 1971 (now titled
Sojourners) and my opportunity to have personal fellowship
with the community out of which it grew, was another startling and hopeful event profoundly encouraging to my spirit.
Their first issue was sent to my office, and I took it home with
me to read over the weekend. Monday morning I tried to
reach them on the phone, not knowing who to call, but assuming that since the mailing address was Deerfield, Illinois,
perhaps they were students at Trinity Seminary, which I knew
to be located there. Finally I reached someone whose name
was on the paper's masthead and simply shared my sense of
enthusiasm and support for what they were trying, in general, to say. Our church was encultured, and our message was
frequently far more an echoing of society's dominant values
rather than a clear proclamation of the whole Gospel, as the
Post-American declared. Here was a group of committed
evangelicals articulating the imperatives of the Gospel for
our time in a compelling biblical fashion. Later, when Jim
Wallis and other members of the community were out in
Washington, we had the opportunity to meet together for discussion, fellowship, and prayer. Such encounters convinced
me that the Spirit was moving in fresh ways through the
evangelical community, prompting many of us to struggle
with fuller understanding of what Christ asks when he calls
us to be his disciples.

There were few people, however, with whom I could honestly share my inner doubts about the wisdom of continuing
in political life, and no one in the Senate, with one notable
exception: Harold Hughes. Harold had become my closest
friend within the Senate. We shared many mutual concerns
and commitments, giving us a basis of communication that
rarely existed between other Senators or other people.

The sense of rapport between us was due not just to our
common Christian commitment, but also to the fact that we
each strove to integrate those convictions into our overall
political philosophy. Harold, like me, was deeply opposed to

the War and concerned about the misguided priorities which
dominate our national life. His faith gave him a deep compassion for the disadvantaged and dispossessed members of
our society, and he placed an ultimate value in the worth
of human life.

Harold Hughes shared my frustration with the seeming
lack of deep purpose in our role as U.S. Senators. The same
questions that were occurring inside my mind filled his mind
also. We both wondered just how much one could be a truly
faithful disciple of Jesus Christ and also be given over fully
to the political process, subject to its influences and priorities.
Together we spent time struggling with these issues. Such
discussion continued through the next two years, when
Hughes decided not to run for re-election.

My whole understanding of leadership and power under-
went a fundamental change as I searched out my future.

Power and prestige could not be the goals which gave
my life a sense of direction or purpose. Those values had to
be relinquished if my commitment was to be authentic. The
purpose of my life is to be faithful to Jesus Christ, to follow
his way, and to be molded according to the imprint of his
life.

No longer could I define leadership in terms of holding
positions of power. Further, power in its truest sense was
not political muscle, influence, and public prestige. I was
coming to a whole new understanding of what power truly
is from a spiritual perspective. Service to others, solely for
their own behalf and even entailing deep sacrifice, is the
true essence of leadership and the ultimate form of power.
There is a power in servanthood which transcends all notions
of power sought after so avidly in the secular political sphere
of life.

All this is evidenced most clearly in the person of Jesus
of Nazareth. Regardless of one's own personal religious beliefs, anyone would have to conclude that this man exercised
a form of power which changed totally the course of history.
Yet what was the nature of that power? What was the style
of his leadership? It was a form of seeming powerlessness,
expressed in self-sacrificial love and service on the behalf

of others. His leadership was the surrendering of his personal prerogatives, the giving up of his ego; it was just the opposite of what the world estimates true leadership to be. His power consisted solely in his radical faithfulness to a vision. He called this vision the "Kingdom of God," and he defined this calling as "doing his Father's will." His method for accomplishing these ends was not to seek public acclaim or devise a calculated strategy, but rather to surrender in utter faithfulness to God's will, exemplifying through a total self-giving love the heart and the message of his mission.

The Christian is committed to molding his or her life to Christ's. We are to seek his power and follow his style of leadership. This means washing another's feet, laying down one's life for his friends, and loving one's enemies. The politician who follows Christ is in no way exempted from obeying "all that has been commanded." He or she is called to be a servant-leader. Self-preservation is no longer the key motive in all political activities; rather, it becomes the service of human need, and prophetic faithfulness to a vision of God's will being done "on earth as it is in heaven."

Radical allegiance to Jesus Christ transforms one's entire perspective on political reality. Priorities become totally changed; a whole new understanding of what is truly important bursts forth. There is an uncompromised identification with the needs of the poor and the oppressed. One is placed in fundamental opposition to structures of injustice and forms of national idolatry. Further, there is a commitment to the power of love as the only means to the end. We are to empty ourselves as he did for the sake of others.

Reconciling such a commitment with daily demands, pressures, and expectations of political life creates constant tension. The temptations and subtle seductions of the world's system of thought exercise a constant power over anyone in the political realm. My own journey has repeatedly revealed the forceful pressures that would conform me to the world's values, keeping me from being transformed, as St. Paul puts it, by the renewing of the Spirit.

Most Americans, and many Christians in America, idolize our political process. The implicit assumption is that our

structures are almost sacred. If a Christian enters the political sphere with concerns about justice at home and
abroad, the priorities of the nation, or other broad social
concerns, then the task usually is seen as reforming the
existing structures to achieve these ends. This is the framework within which I began to bring my Christian faith into
relationship with my "progressive" political perspectives.

As I have endeavored to confront more directly the mandate of the Gospel and its relationship to political reality in
America, I have found this approach to be less and less a
viable alternative. First, my political and philosophical understanding of our nation's problems convinces me that the
mere reform of existing structures will not adequately address the problems we face. Certain short-term improve-
ments and measures to alleviate human need can be wrought,
to be sure. But these typically amount to applying Band-Aids
on wounds for which major surgery is needed.

Second, in some ways, our political system does adequately
represent the people of America as it works its will; the
problem is not the system, but rather, the people themselves,
and their values. Militarism and foreign intervention abroad
are only in part a function of powerful bureaucratic and
economic forces; they also grow from the values of most
Americans. The thought that we can achieve domestic and
global justice just by reforming our political structures
assumes that the majority of Americans desire such justice,
and all that it actually demands, risks, or entails of us. That
is highly questionable.

As I understand biblical truth about the conflict between
the way of faith and the way of the world, the conclusions
just cited are not deeply surprising. Power is organized in
the world around the world's values. Our culture's values
express a materialistic, and even pagan, ethic. Wealth and
status are worshiped and dominate, in many ways, the
decision-making in our institutions. As our structures are
shaped by those values, they naturally become less capable
of working for the needs of the poor and oppressed. Thus,
our political structures and institutions fall under God's
judgment; they are in rebellion, afflicted by the Fall, re-

flecting corporately the sin that lies within the hearts of men and women. That does not mean they are incapable of doing any good; in relative terms, of course they can. There are always possibilities for attempting to nudge or coerce the structures of power into some measure of response to higher values. We should strive for those works of partial and relative justice which may be wrought from our system. Yet, we should realize that if achieved, these are exceptions, and providential works of grace. The Christian cannot place all hope for the liberation of humanity from oppression in gradual reforms wrought by our political institutions.

I have come to see more clearly the prophetic role any Christian is called upon to exercise within our political realm. Our witness within the political order must hold fast, with uncompromised allegiance, to the vision of the New Order proclaimed by Christ. Our allegiance and hope rest fundamentally with his power, at work in the world through his Spirit, rather than in the efficacy of our world's systems and structures to bring about social righteousness in the eyes of God. Any assumption that the movement of the Spirit and dominant direction of our political institutions are always the same must be utterly rejected. When St. Paul asserts that Christians struggle against "principalities and powers," this includes the powers inherent in the political structures ruling over us. The prophetic role exposes the true nature of these powers, points to God's judgment upon them, and proclaims for all who will hear the hopeful imperatives of justice, righteousness, and peace as set forth by God, and expressed through the life of his Son. A posture of servanthood, conformed to the image of Christ's life, must accompany such a witness.

As this vision of servanthood emerged with greater clarity, the decision about my future was cast in an entirely different light. Remaining in politics at all costs could never be the purpose of my life. Rather, the sphere of politics was simply one avenue for trying, as best I could, to be a faithful follower of my Lord and his Kingdom. There was no assurance that I could win my election or succeed according to the terms of the political world. But that precisely was what did

not ultimately matter. Endeavoring to live as a faithful disciple was the first call of my life, rather than striving for
what society defined as success.

In the late fall of 1971 I went home to Newport, Oregon,
with my wife for a weekend. For many hours I merely walked
along the beach, looking at the sea and the sky as I tried to
collect my thoughts and prayers. During that weekend I
decided to run for re-election to the Senate. I would seek
to stay where I was and see if I could remain true to the
larger call and vision that I had accepted on my life.
Political factors entered into the choice scarcely at all. I
would work hard in the campaign for re-election, but would
then accept the result, whatever it was, as being right for
my life. There was a deep sense of relinquishment. I began
to feel liberated from the idolatry of power and given over
more deeply to a whole new vision of prophetic witness,
faithfulness, and servanthood.

Chapter 3

Prophetic Faithfulness

IN EARLY August of 1971, I received the minutes of the Young Life Executive Committee of their National Board of Directors. As a member of that Board, I was especially concerned about one crucial issue:

SMITTY FLYNN MATTER

President Bill Starr advised the Executive Committee that Young Life staff member, Smitty Flynn, who is Area Director in Birmingham, Alabama, has been opposed to the war in Vietnam. In furtherance of that protest, he has turned in his draft card. Because of this action, Southeastern Regional Director Roy Riviere released Smitty Flynn from the Young Life staff. Mr. Starr indicated that he has deferred final action in dismissing Smitty from the staff in order that the Executive Committee could consider the question of civil disobedience and whether or not the umbrella of Young Life was large enough to include staff men who have taken this type of action.

Mr. Starr made available correspondence from Smitty Flynn, as well as a positional statement on civil disobedience concurred by Dr. Paul K. Jewett, Dean of the Young Life Institute, and Dr. Vernon Grounds, faculty member of the Institute.

Committee Member Marvin Heaps made the following observations concerning this issue:

—The Young Life umbrella is broad enough to include a conscientious objector, if this position is dictated by a man's Christian conscience.
—Young Life cannot condone a criminal act, nor can Young Life condone any action which impairs and hinders the primary task of Young Life, which is the proclamation of the Gospel.
—In no event should Smitty Flynn have taken this action unilaterally without first counselling with the appropriate Young Life staff men and advising top management of what he intended to do.

At the conclusion of extensive discussion, the Committee concluded unanimously that the action of Roy Riviere in releasing Smitty Flynn from the Young Life staff should be affirmed, unless Smitty would be willing to do the following:
   A. Request that his draft card be reissued to him without in any way recanting his position on the Vietnam war;
   B. Share his views as to the reasons for his actions with members of the Young Life family.[1]

Such concrete circumstances focus our theological and philosophical convictions about issues in a way that mere intellectual musing never does. This was such a case for myself, and many others involved.

It was a rare and startling event for a committed evangelical Christian to express his opposition to the War so fervently that it could lead to an act of civil disobedience. The evangelical consensus about the rightness of the War was being questioned by only a small minority; most all evangelicals, even if they had private misgivings about past policies, found it difficult to break their allegiance to President Nixon. It was easier to believe all rhetoric about negotiations, withdrawing some of the troops, and achieving a "peace with honor," in spite of the escalating bombing and expanding war.

Even stronger, however, was the almost unquestioned assumption of the Christian's unqualified duty to obey the State. Viewed in that light, the position statement on civil disobedience prepared by Dr. Paul Jewett of Fuller Seminary, and Dean of the Young Life Institute, must have come as a shock to many on the Board and elsewhere who read it:

STATEMENT ON CIVIL DISOBEDIENCE
Young Life Campaign

By: Doctors Paul K. Jewett, Vernon Grounds, James Martin, George Kelsey, John Stam, and Messrs. James Malcolm, Paul Borgman, concurring.

1. The Christian is a citizen of the kingdom of heaven and, in this life, also of a particular country.
2. The Christian, therefore, recognizes his obligation to obey God and the civil magistrate, the state being an ordinance of God, which, in a fallen society, has the power of the sword to preserve justice (Rom. 13).
3. Because man is sinful, the ideal of perfect justice is only relatively attained in any state. The Christian, therefore, has the obligation to obey the civil authority even in a state that is not as just as it ought to be. It is only in those situations where the requirements of the state are so grossly unjust as to compel a Christian to deny his citizenship in the kingdom of heaven, that he is obliged to obey God rather than man. Examples of such civil disobedience are found both in Scripture and in subsequent church history. The following may be cited:
   a. The three Hebrew children who defied Nebuchadnezzar's orders to bow before an image (Dan. 3) and Daniel's refusal to heed the decree of Darius (Dan. 6).
   b. The refusal of the apostles to obey the order of the Sanhedrin to desist from all Christian witness (Acts 4:18–20).
   c. Many early martyrs who went to their death rather than burn incense to the image of the emperor, betray the

secret of where their Scriptures were hidden, or deny that Jesus was Lord.

d. Those who died for their right to worship God according to the dictates of their own conscience before, during, and after the Protestant Reformation.

e. In more recent times, those in Nazi Germany, who, as members of the Confessing Church, signed the Barmen Declaration and sought to overthrow Hitler, particularly because of his discrimination against the Jews.

f. Those in our own land who, before and during the Civil War, aided and abetted slaves in escaping from their masters or refused to return escaped slaves to their masters, all such activity being illegal and contrary to the laws of the land.

g. Those in present-day America who have disobeyed various civil ordinances, like Rosa Parks of Montgomery, Alabama, who refused to surrender her bus seat to a white passenger, as the law required. In this she was widely supported by Christian churches, especially in the black community.

A review of these and other examples of civil disobedience by Christians indicates that there are "boundary situations" in which the civil authority seeks to impose a manifest injustice in the state by denying to citizens those God-given freedoms which belong to them as men.

One cannot say that Christians have always resisted such injustice nor that they have always improved society when they have so resisted. One can only say that Christians have the right so to resist, that sometimes they have insisted on this right as a witness to the truth, as God has given them to see the truth, and that the injustice, as well as the protest, varies with the circumstances.

Further, it must be admitted that, because of these varying circumstances, Christians have not always agreed as to when they should disobey the civil magistrate and what expression their disobedience should take. The case of the apostles, who chose to obey God rather than men in the matter of preaching Christ, is a clear instance concerning which all would agree that their act was morally right, though illegal in the sense that it defied the order of Israel's highest authority, the Sanhedrin. However, it is not sufficient to say that the Christian is free to disobey the civil magistrate only when he finds himself in a situation identical to that of the apostles. Scripture examples of right action are given to illumine a larger truth; in this case, the larger truth that the Christian owes ultimate allegiance to God and not to the state.

The Christian community, therefore, has always reflected general agreement on the right of civil disobedience, but has disagreed on circumstances calling for such disobedience and the extent to which it may go. Such disagreement has especially marked the attitude of the Christian community toward war. The majority of Christians have participated in war, some with good conscience, some with doubts. Others have refused all participation except that of a non-combatant. Still others have refused to participate even in this limited way, either because they regarded war in general as incompatible with a Christian confession or because they were convinced that a particular war was unjust and immoral.

Obviously all these positions cannot be equally right, but in questions of conscience, wherein Christians differ, we should respect the scruples of a brother, even when we do not agree with him (1 Cor. 8). It is likewise the obligation of one who in conscience differs from the majority of his brethren to realize that the liberty which they have granted him to dissent carries with it the responsibility to face the consequence of his decision whatever these consequences may be. It should also be remembered that granting one the liberty of dissent, does not necessarily mean approval of his dissent.

Finally, it is to be admitted that the consequence of civil disobedience may be very serious, as in extreme cases of conspiracy and violent revolution. There would seem to be very few times in history when the Christian could have any part in such radical civil disobedience.

On the other hand, to deny all civil disobedience to Christians would have even more serious consequences, since it would imply that the authority of the state is absolute and its laws identical with the will of God. This is to make the state a total state and to threaten the loss of all Christian and democratic freedoms. It is because the state has demonic possibilities (note the figure of "Babylon" in the Apocalypse of John 18) that one should not base his theology of the state solely on Romans 13. *The state, according to the New Testament, is both the ordinance of God and an instrument of Satan.*

Addendum on Violence and Non-Violence

Instances of exceptional cases in which Christians were involved in violent acts of civil disobedience would be the Huguenot Wars of Religion in France, the overthrow of the Spanish by the Dutch Calvinists under William of Orange, the Puritan uprising against the English Crown under Cromwell, and our own American Revolution which protested the injustice of taxation without representation.

If the Christian community allows the possibility that Christians may rightfully have participated in such acts of violent civil disobedience—and the majority does so allow—then surely we should be tolerant toward those acts of civil disobedience which are non-violent in nature, when done for the sake of conscience.

This is not to say that conscience is an infallible guide, nor to deny that a given violent act of civil disobedience may commend itself as warranted by Scripture (by whose authority we seek to resolve all questions of conscience) above a given non-violent act of civil disobedience. We are saying only that as a general principle violent resistance to the civil magistrate is more problematical for the Christian than non-violent resistance, in the light of the teaching of Scripture about the nature of the kingdom of heaven and Jesus' own life style as reported in the Gospels.

Many times I have thought about what I would have done if I had been an eligible draftee during the Vietnam War. I had fought with the Navy in World War II and its aftermath when, in fact, we ended up in Hanoi, just liberated from Japanese occupation. Ho Chi Minh had set up his government, backed with extremely widespread nationalistic sentiment; war against the French, who attempted to reimpose colonial rule, had not yet begun. But now, twenty-five years later, I realized my conscience would never have allowed me to go back and fight in Indochina. That would have violated not only my conscience, but my faith.

I had not examined, however, in any careful biblical, historical and theological way the Christian's relationship to the State, particularly in light of my personal convictions. The case of Smitty Flynn gave me that opportunity. Bill

Starr had suggested that the entire question be discussed at the full meeting of Young Life's Board later that year, in December.

The task of studying these questions with care and in depth seemed enormous. I discussed this with a trusted staff member, and we decided to contact two former interns in my office, who were now seminary students, for assistance. Focusing first on Old and New Testament teachings that would shed light on the Christian's relation to the State, we would then examine historically what has occurred, in at least a summary manner, in the relations of the Christian community with the governing authorities. In this way, I hoped to gain a deeper biblical and historical background from which to examine convictions about the Christian and the State in our present time.

Trying to articulate these thoughts four years later, I recognize fully that I am not an academic scholar either of biblical teaching or the history of the Church. But I have tried to understand these matters as best I can, keeping my mind and heart open to new perspectives. By now a whole range of articles and books has been published exploring these questions, frequently with greater depth and scholarly expertise than I could ever hope to offer. Many such writers, in fact, have played major roles in influencing my own convictions on these issues.

Let me offer, then, a summary of what I discovered as I responded to the matter confronting Young Life's Board in 1971. The study I began then is in no way complete, of course, and continues today.

The Old Testament, we must realize, reveals that the government of the children of Israel was a theocracy, based on a unique covenant between God and his chosen people. Faithfulness to it involved living in obedience to God's revelation and leading, as given in the Law and expressed by the prophets. Since all Israelites, rulers and commoners alike, were pledged to the covenant, it is impossible to draw a direct analogy between the Israelite's relationship to his or her rulers and the relationship of the Christian toward a secular modern State.

Occasionally, there are attempts to formulate just such a direct analogy—America becomes the "promised land" with a special covenant relationship to God. But that is simply not the case. Believing that our nation has a special dispensation of God's blessing as opposed, for instance, to Norway or Tanzania or Yugoslavia, simply confuses any biblical understanding of God's relationship to our nation and the world. God is not choosing special peoples over others in the modern world as he chose the people of Israel, nor giving them a particular, unique covenant involving faithfulness to his promises.

Nevertheless, the Old Testament can still teach us about God's standards of justice for any people and any nation, and the accountability of earthly powers to these exacting standards. In this way, the Old Testament does have a direct and poignant relevance to the Christian's relationship toward America, or any modern secular State.

The people of Israel understood Yahweh, the Lord, as their King, the Lord over their history. Yahweh promised to lead the children of Abraham to the Promised Land, and to establish a Kingdom of justice and righteousness; but the people were called to remain faithful to the Law he had given them. This was the covenant between Yahweh and his people.

All earthly forms of political authority were to be held accountable to this covenant relationship. Initially, this meant that the children of Israel would not have a king as other peoples did, for Yahweh alone was the Ruler. As the Israelites began to turn with curiosity and then envy to neighboring peoples, they began to adopt some of their ways. Eventually, they too wanted an earthly king. Samuel finally assented and anointed Saul. However, he gave the Israelites this warning, which has a wider relevance to any desire of a people for kingly, authoritarian power to reign over them:

Samuel told the people who were asking him for a king all that the Lord had said to him. "This will be the sort of king who will govern you," he said. "He will take your sons and make them serve in his chariots and with his cavalry, and will make them run before his chariot. Some he will appoint officers over units of a thousand and units of fifty. Others will plough his fields and reap his harvest; others again will make weapons of war and equipment for mounted troops. He will take your daughters for perfumers, cooks, and confectioners, and will seize the best of your cornfields, vineyards, and oliveyards, and give them to his lackeys. He will take a tenth of your grain and your vintage to give to his eunuchs and lackeys. Your slaves, both men and women, and the best of your cattle and your asses he will seize and put to his own use. He will take a tenth of your flocks, and you yourselves will become his slaves. When that day comes, you will cry out against the king whom you have chosen; but it will be too late, the Lord will not answer you" (1 Sam. 8:10–19).

Once the monarchy was established, however, the role of Israel's kings was understood distinctly in light of the covenant, and reflected the continual tension between the demands of that covenant and the realities in Israel's history. The kings, like the judges, were to be the humble servants of the people and of Yahweh, upholding his Law. Their rule, and all authority in Israel's life, was understood not as the opportunity for exploitation and aggrandizement, but as the means for promoting faithfulness to Yahweh's Law and compliance with the will of the Lord.

But Israel's political, economic, and social institutions, however, continually fell short of true faithfulness to the covenant. God's prophets spoke his Word and called the people back to faithfulness, revealing to the Israelites the unfaithfulness manifest in their corporate life and institutions. The prophets' message, then, was actually a proclamation of Yahweh's lordship over history, his promise to establish a kingdom of righteousness, and therefore, the Lord's severe judgment on the rebellion and sin that had come to dominate Israel's life.

Jeremiah succinctly expresses the mandate of the prophets:

"For to all to whom I send you, you shall go, and whatever I command you, you shall speak. . . . Behold, I have put my

words in your mouth. See, I have set you this day over nations
and over kingdoms, to pluck up and to break down, to destroy
and to overthrow, to build and to plant" (Jer. 1:7, 9–10, RSV).

How is their word relevant to us today?

It seems obvious that we can view their words as address-
ing not simply Israel, but in a larger sense, pointing out the
standards of justice and righteousness God demands within
any corporate society. The prophets were speaking out of
a future promised to Israel by the Lord in the covenant;
with the coming of Jesus Christ as the Messiah, however,
we discover that God's promised future for Israel becomes
his promise to all the world. Its fulfillment will become a
complete reality at the end of time, when Christ establishes
his Kingdom, which shall have no end. In this present time,
then, our world stands accountable to God's standards of
justice and righteousness, and to the Lord's words of judgment as expressed first to the people of Israel through the
prophets. Modern states do not possess individually a self-
conscious Old Testament covenant relationship with God,
nor hold a special promise from him for the future of their
people, as did ancient Israel. But we can examine our own
national life, and that of other nations, in light of God's
Word; further, we can also understand from the prophets
a model for how the servant of God is to relate to political
power.

Old Testament scholar James Muilenburg, in *The Way
of Israel,* suggests five major areas addressed by the prophets.[2]
Examining each of these briefly may help us better understand their message and any potential application to our
own situation.

First, the prophets courageously confronted the whole
structure of political life in Israel. They warned against the
whole idea of adopting earthly kings because that threatened
to undermine the rule of Yahweh over his people. They saw
the need to trust in earthly, conventional forms of political
power as a sign of a profound distrust in the Lord of history
by his chosen people. The prophets understood, percep-
tively and correctly, that the world's political power struc-

tures are invariably corrupted by their own necessity for
self-justification and self-maintenance. Those who held positions of kingship would inevitably "lord it over others," as
Christ himself said, rather than submit to be the Lord's
humble and faithful servants.

Once earthly kingship was an established part of Israel's
political order, the prophets went before the kings, continually proclaiming the limits to their sovereignty and the
actual, ultimate rule of Yahweh over history and over all
earthly designs of kingship and political power.

Second, the prophets demonstrated a deep and sharp concern over economic injustice in Israelite society. As that
society evolved from a wandering, nomadic existence to a
stable, urbanized society, an inequitable distribution of
wealth reflective of our own time began to characterize it.
The Law provided the people of Israel with an uncompromised mandate to care for the poor, the defenseless, and
the oppressed of society. The vision of social order it spelled
out, in fact, provided that there would be none in deep need
among their number.

This mandate was pushed out of consciousness as mercan-
tilism invaded Israelite culture. Classes began to emerge,
and Israel's rulers and merchants began to be obsessed by
personal greed and search for profit. Commercial structures
exploited the poor. Rulers and wealthy allied to preserve this
economic order, with all of its injustice. In their eyes, the
economy, gaining new wealth from foreign markets, was
sound and profitable; but it was not so for the dispossessed,
and for the people as a whole. The prophets, unwilling to
accept any of the rationalizations laced with national pride
and the quest for wealth that lay behind the economic system, spoke out. Amos's indictment is typically strong:

Hear this, you who trample upon the needy! Therefore because you trample upon the poor and take from him exactions
of wheat, you have built houses of hewn stone, but you shall
not dwell in them; you have planted pleasant vineyards, but
you shall not drink their wine. For I know how many are your
transgressions, and how great are your sins—you who afflict the

righteous, who take a bribe, and turn aside the needy in the gate (Amos 5:11–12, RSV).

A third area of the prophets' concern, according to Muilenburg and other Old Testament scholars, was the stewardship of the land. In a unique sense, the land was given in trust by Yahweh to the *whole* people. Both individually—for land was held privately by individuals—and corporately, the people were to be caretakers of the land for its ultimate and true owner—Yahweh; and its productivity and fruitfulness were related to their social righteousness. As they transgressed and disregarded the Law, they were then violating their trust as stewards of the land as well.

Fourth, the prophets condemned the administration of justice in Israel. The Law and the Deuteronomic Code gave to the people of Israel an absolute standard of impartiality in the administration of justice. But this was ignored as the courts increasingly served to protect the privileged from the oppressed, and laws were written which intensified the exploitation of the poor. Such law and its authors came under Isaiah's condemnation: "What will you do on the day of punishment, in the storm which will come from afar? To whom will you flee for help, and where will you leave your wealth?" (Isa. 10:3).

Finally, the prophets reveal their deep distrust of power. Neither open nor accountable to any judgment, it receives the stinging judgment of the Lord. Even though the king was supposed to be the chosen one of the Lord, the prophets spared no polite respect or deference in their frequent face-to-face confrontations over the misuse of the rulers' power. Isaiah's words offer sweeping judgment:

> For the Lord has a day against all that is proud and lofty, against all that is lifted up and high; against all the cedars of Lebanon, lofty and lifted up; and against all the oaks of Bashan; against all the high mountains, and against all the lofty hills; against every high tower, and against every fortified wall; against all the ships of Tarshish, and against all the beautiful craft. And the haughtiness of man shall be humbled,

and the pride of men shall be brought low; and the Lord alone
will be exalted in that day (Isa. 2:12–17, RSV).

We can apply these prophetic perspectives as standards of
judgment relevant to any nation-state. Note that the prophets
did not advocate moderate means for reforming their political structures. Theirs was not the approach of Common
Cause. Rather, the prophetic Word they spoke focused on
the radical expectations of God for his people, and his
displeasure with those institutions and governments which
seemed, without exception, to thwart his hopes because of
their own vested interests and lack of faithfulness. God's
Word through his prophets concerning justice, the treatment of the poor, the pretensions of power, and other aspects
of national life, was not tailored as a simple appeal to make
good institutions better ones, nor was it couched in terms
making it more acceptable to those listening. Rather, it was
a call to repentance, to faithfulness to God rather than to
earthly realities—a call to the hope of God's promises to
those who respond to his Lordship and mercy.

In some instances the response to the prophetic Word did
result in acts of partial reform within existing structures, although such reforms usually were negated by subsequent
unfaithfulness. On other occasions, the powers ignored the
prophetic Word, and cast out those who spoke it. Yet, despite
such hardness of heart, the Word of the Lord still addressed
his people, taking root wherever there was some openness
of spirit, and interjecting itself as a presence in the life of
the society. Because the prophetic Word had a life and a
power of its own, it did not need to be allied with the destiny
of Israel's political institutions, and was free to speak a clear
word of truth and judgment.

God's Word today to the nations of the world, in my understanding, possesses the same kind of relevance as did the
prophetic Word of the Old Testament. Obviously, since
as Americans we are not a people living in a self-conscious
covenant relationship with God, his Word to our nation and
our structures of government is in no way allied to their

perpetuation. Rather it comes with a clarity of judgment
on the present order, and with a hope born only of repentance. This situation, however, is in no way unique to our
modern age. It evolved in the Old Testament and characterized God's relationship to the people of Israel, who had
thoroughly forsaken his way by the time that he sent his Son,
the Messiah, as the full embodiment of his Word and Life.

As the people of Israel continued in increasing acts of
unfaithfulness to the Lord, the prophets came to realize
that God's Kingdom and Rule over his people could in no
way be equated with the present nation-state of their time.
The Israelite nation was increasingly choosing an identity
that was severed from its Covenant with their Lord; thus,
the prophetic Word was heard increasingly as judgment on
that order. The hope set forth for Israel rested first with an
ideal State, to be established by God's initiative, brought
into being by his Messiah. Thus, the people began to look
to each of their kings as being the potential leader for a
wholly new nation-state, whose emergence would be in sharp
discontinuity with the old order. This hope, however, was
still laden with a nationalistic delusion of an indestructible
earthly State that would embody the Kingdom of God.

In Isaiah, the messianic expectation became linked to
God's coming judgment, which would leave a purified Remnant of his people. The hope for God's Kingdom moved
from the nation-state to the faithful Remnant of God's
people left among the children of Abraham. Thus God's
promises began to be understood as given not to any manifestation of the State, which remained judged by its unfaithfulness, but rather to those people—to that Remnant—who
are set aside from Israel as the faithful people of God.

To this setting comes the witness of the prophet Jeremiah.
As the Old Testament teacher John Bright says in *The Kingdom of God*, "Jeremiah's message is, of course, a total rejection of the State as the vehicle of the Kingdom of God beyond
which nothing could be more total." [3] Jeremiah, as well as
Ezekiel, saw the State totally in rebellion against God, and
virtually at war with him. Not only was Jeremiah devastating in his condemnation of the nation-state and its institu-

tions, which he compared to a wild beast which had turned against God,[4] but he also failed even to find a spiritual Remnant within Israel. The sin and idolatry of the nation and its people was so total that even the hope of a saving Remnant was devastated by this prophetic Word. He tells us that a single honest person cannot be found, for the sin and unfaithfulness of the society has permeated all. It is not surprising that Jeremiah's message meant for him social and political persecution, denunciation as a traitor, and imprisonment. Yet Jeremiah still held forth a hope in the Lord, and in his ultimate faithfulness and mercy.

This hope set forth by Jeremiah's prophetic Word was in a "new covenant" which had to take root within the hearts of men and women: "But this is the covenant. . . . I will set my law within them, and write it on their hearts; I will become their God, and they shall become my people" (Jer. 31:33–34).

The uniqueness of this message is the futility of external reforms, or hopes in the improvement of the present, worldly dominated order, to mitigate the judgment of God. It is not that such reformist efforts should be totally abandoned; rather, it is to warn against any naive hope in their ability to diminish the absoluteness of God's judgment, and to caution against the futility of seeking such one-dimensional action, aimed only at externals, without recognizing the utter pervasiveness and power of corporate sin in society to poison all its members. Such a call involves relinquishing our own ideas of our ability to control and manipulate history.

In the face of the vision painted by Jeremiah, our response must be one of faith in the Lord's reign, rather than in our mastery of history, which has proven so disastrous. Jeremiah's word of hope beyond the judgment was in the creation of a new people, a people liberated from the corrosive sin of their society through the radical transformation of God's Spirit from within. Such a people live under a New Covenant, holding forth the hope of God's Kingdom, and in fundamental opposition to the old order which languishes without hope under the crushing weight of its sins. Jere-

miah's prophetic Word reaches forth to its fulfillment in
the Word made flesh. But it also gives us a biblical understanding of our situation as Christians in our own day. The
word we hear may seem totally foreign to the values and
outlook of secular culture; but we should recall it sounded
no less extreme to those who first heard it.

God's Word in the Old Testament, spoken through his
prophets, is not completed with Jeremiah. Rather, the New
Covenant he spoke of is given shape and made all the more
sharp and discontinuous with the prevailing understanding
of the culture, in the latter part of Isaiah's witness. There
we hear the word of a new event to come about through the
action of God in faithfulness to his promises. Part of God's
new work is the vision that his domain stretches throughout
the whole world. God's Kingdom is severed from any identification with the nation-state of the people of Israel; more
than that, it is understood as reaching out to include those
from all nations who turn to the Lord. God's totality of judgment on the old order held forth a startling new hope.

We then learn of the shape of this new event. It will be
wrought through a "Suffering Servant," the Messiah, in
struggle with the world, and finally victorious over it. The
dynamics of his action are suffering and death. In his mission
lies the only true fulfillment of the people of Israel, and the
only hope of humankind. Those faithful to the God of
Abraham, Isaac, and Jacob are called to this same mission.
The people of God become a Remnant who are the people
of his Suffering Servant. Their posture of servanthood is the
very means through which God's purposes are wrought.
These new people find their life and hope through their
identity with the outpouring, sacrificial love of the Suffering Servant; his way is to be their own.

The New Covenant first set forth by Jeremiah takes this
dramatic shape, and in its self-giving mission lies the only
hope of all the nations. God's final victory is assured through
his Messiah as this Suffering Servant, and those who, as
God's people, are called in faithfulness to his mission. His
struggle with the rebellion of the world's order becomes
theirs, and his suffering love becomes one with them.

Chapter 4

The Politics of the Cross

THE OUTSET of this decade in America was marked with draft resistance, massive protests against war, estrangement from the political process, and strong dissent from America's domestic and foreign polices. Still, most Christians were reluctant to believe that Jesus Christ had any concrete relevance to such issues, even though they knew Christ as their inward personal Savior. Yet they had not grasped the truth that his life was lived, like ours, amidst social upheaval, and that he was deeply involved in the struggles of his society. Christ's witness spoke powerfully to his disciples about the political, social, and economic tensions they confronted in their age. His words and teachings, I have come to believe, are no less relevant to similar questions raised in our world today.

Jesus was born into a time and land torn by political

unrest. The people of Israel lived under the occupation of Rome. Bitterness toward Roman rule ran deep, erupting often into armed rebellion. Historians tell us that in the year Jesus was born, a major armed uprising against the Romans occurred, only to be crushed when Varus, the Governor of Syria, came to Jerusalem with two legions of soldiers and proceeded to crucify two thousand of the rebels.

When Jesus was about ten, Roman rule became more pervasive over his country, with strict taxes levied on the people and the land's economic resources. The most adamant in their resistance were the Zealots, who believed that Israel had to remain totally loyal to the Law and to Yahweh as its only Lord. For them, this entailed violence against the occupying Romans as well as against Israelites who collaborated with Roman rulers. The Zealots steadfastly resisted paying taxes of tribute to Rome, one of their chief popular points of contention.

A fervent messianic hope was held forth by the Zealots; yet it was laden with the strident nationalism which prophets before their time had utterly condemned. For the Zealots, the Messiah would be the one who would successfully lead their revolt against Rome, re-establishing the political power of Israel and then ruling over the nations, as foretold. Like modern-day leaders of national liberation movements, struggling against oppression and wholeheartedly committed to the righteousness of their cause, the Zealots saw violent revolution as the only means to bring in a new and purified political order.

Against the background of Old Testament history, the Zealots heard clearly the demands of their Lord for uncompromised allegiance to him, and him alone. They were following in the tradition of those prophets who condemned the injustice of rulers who sought after their own power and spurned Yahweh. But they failed to hear the tradition of prophetic judgment against their own self-righteous, nationalistic pretensions. For the Zealots, Israel as a nation-state could still be redeemed, even if through the shedding of blood. It was not, however, blood of the Suffering Servant and his means of self-giving love, but rather the blood of those slain by a religious war of independence and liberation.

Other prominent political and religious groups took a markedly different approach. One powerful faction was the Pharisees. As religious leaders, the Pharisees demanded rigid observance of the letter of the Law and a strict religious purity. However, they saw their religion as only applying to a limited, "spiritual" sphere of life; there was little relevance to the broader political realities of the whole society. The Pharisees were legalists whose myopic concentration on religiosity destroyed social conscience and prophetic vision. Although they possessed nationalistic, anti-Roman sentiments, they offered no fundamental challenge to Roman authority and power, no forthright condemnation of its oppression and injustice. As long as their own religious establishment was able to function, the Pharisees, despite their strong misgivings, were content to live with Roman rule and not become involved in "politics."

The Sadducees went even further. They collaborated masterfully with the Roman occupiers, seeking to build a religious-political alliance. In exchange, they received the support of the Roman authorities for their own undertakings but lost touch totally with the prophetic tradition of the Old Testament. The Sadducees simply set aside any messianic hope for God's Kingdom in favor of dealing "realistically" with the pragmatic realities of power which confronted them.

Jesus Christ, the Incarnate Word of God, lived within this concrete political environment. We can find guidance, I believe, for deciding how the Christian should relate to political power through understanding the way our Lord responded to the concrete political options which faced his own life.

First, it is clear that Christ was uncompromising in his judgment of the Pharisees—their hypocrisy, their self-righteousness, and their system of legalistic religiosity. Some of his very harshest rebukes were directed against the Pharisees; he would have no part of a sterile religiosity which was segregated from life. The Pharisees "overlooked the weightier demands of the Law, justice, mercy, and good faith" (Matt. 23:23) and were thus without any meaningful social conscience, along with all the other items of the stinging indictment Christ presents in Matthew 23.

The Sadducees, in like manner, came under Christ's judgment. He rejected their position and strongly condemned the existing religious-political establishment. Jesus announced that the present order was incompatible with the Kingdom of God and its demands. When he called tax collectors like Matthew to follow him, they had to give up their former life of involvement with the injustices of Roman power. Jesus could not tolerate the collaboration of the Sadducees, for it totally contradicted allegiance to the Kingdom of God with its values and promised future.

In the context of his own time, Christ could only have been considered an opponent and a threat to the existing political and religious establishment. So it was that the Sadducees, the Pharisees, and the Roman officials together all conspired to put him to death.

What, then, was his relationship to the Zealots? Jesus had regular contact with the Zealots and their followers. In fact, there were Zealots among the twelve disciples. One disciple is specifically identified as "Simon the Zealot," and Judas Iscariot could well have been part of the movement. Biblical scholars believe that the sons of Zebedee as well as Simon Peter might also have been Zealots or their allies.[1] The attraction of the Zealots to Jesus is understandable, for they agreed with his opposition to the religious-political establishment of the day. After all, Jesus expelled the religious entrepreneurs from the temple, he called Herod a fox (Luke 13:22), and he spoke against kings who oppressed the people (Luke 22:25).

Christ, though, refused to embrace the means advocated by the Zealots to achieve their end. He knew that the fulfillment of God's promises to his people lay not in a violent rebellion to expel the Romans and establish a new Jewish theocracy. Rather, it was found in the way of the Suffering Servant.

In this light we can understand far better the drama of Christ's confrontation with the Pharisees and others over the question of paying taxes to Caesar.

Then the Pharisees went away and agreed on a plan to trap him in his own words. Some of their followers were sent to him in company with men of Herod's party. They said, "Master, you are an honest man, we know; you teach in all honesty the way of life that God requires, truckling to no man, whoever he may be. Give us your ruling on this: are we or are we not permitted to pay taxes to the Roman Emperor?" Jesus was aware of their malicious intention and said to them, "You hypocrites! Why are you trying to catch me out? Show me the money in which the tax is paid." They handed him a silver piece. Jesus said, "Whose head is this, and whose inscription?" "Caesar's," they replied. He said to them, "Then pay Caesar what is due to Caesar, and pay God what is due to God." This answer took them by surprise, and they went away and left him alone (Matt. 22:15–22).

We must remember that this was no serious inquiry into the theology of God and the State, put forth by faithful disciples, but a cunningly designed dilemma, part of a conspiracy to "trap" Jesus, so that he would play into the hands of at least one of the rival factions. Those who asked the question were not interested at all in the truth of this matter, but were intent only on the destruction of Christ. If he answered plainly in the negative, he would be branded as a revolutionary Zealot. The "men from King Herod's party," who were one of the groups posing the question, might have even arrested him. If he answered unequivocally in the positive, he would have been discredited before the people as a collaborationist. Certainly anyone whom people were acclaiming as the Messiah could not advocate collaboration with the oppressive rule of Rome. Christ's answer, however, satisfied no one. Rather, they were "astonished" when he said, "Render therefore to Caesar the things that are Caesar's, and to God the things that are God's" (Matt. 22:21, rsv).

Crucial to the passage is the notion that what is due

Caesar, and only what is due him, should be rendered back
to him. According to those who study the original Greek
of the New Testament, the word chosen by Jesus, translated
as "render" or "give back," means the handing over of that
which is already owed as a debt. The implication is that
there is a legitimate obligation which government can ask
of its citizens, but one with its boundaries sharply circumscribed. We are to give to Caesar only that which is due as
his. Then, we are to give to God all that is due as his. And
what is that? A few verses later Christ makes it clear in
summarizing the Law: " 'Love the Lord your God with all
your heart, with all your soul, with all your mind.' That is
the greatest commandment. It comes first" (Matt. 22:37–38).

Our heresy today comes in believing that the spheres of
Caesar and God are equal, or that they can never make
conflicting claims on the Christian. That is not at all the
meaning of Christ's words. In asking for a denarius, he asked
for a coin which bears the inscription of Caesar. According
to rabbinic instruction, possession of such a coin was not
allowed; because of the graven image, it acknowledged a
form of idolatry. Christ exposed the hypocrisy of the Pharisees by requesting such a coin, which at least some in their
number carried, and asking pointedly whose image it bears.
The coin, bearing Caesar's image and claimed by him,
should be rendered to him. But the person, bearing the
image of God, and claimed by him, should be given over
wholly to his Service.

Jesus Christ came proclaiming the good news of the Kingdom of God. That proclamation must be understood in its
full political and spiritual sense.

When Mary received the word that she was to bear the
Son of God, she proclaimed the Hymn of Praise—The Mag-
nificat—which reads in part:

"He has shown strength with his arm,
he has scattered the proud in the imagination of their hearts,
he has put down the mighty from their thrones,
and exalted those of low degree;

he has filled the hungry with good things,
and the rich he has sent empty away" (Luke 1:51–53, RSV).

The call for radical change within society is interwoven with
the proclamation of the coming of the Lord. The political
and the social implications of the incarnation are present
from the very moment of Christ's conception within Mary.

This same truth is shown at the birth of Christ. Matthew
tells us that Christ, when just an infant, was already viewed
as a threat by the political and religious establishment. King
Herod took the word of foreign astrologers so seriously, and
was so fearful of one who could call into question his power
and his authority, that he ordered a massacre of infants. Jesus'
parents fled with him from their land because of this political
persecution.

When we study the Gospels carefully, we see that there
is no foundation for assuming that the true spiritual significance of Christ as Messiah and as our Savior in any way
negates the radical political and social consequences of his
incarnation, life, death and resurrection. We see that in the
words of John the Baptist, who, as the preparer of the Way
of the Lord, called for social repentance, both individual and
corporate. Listen to the words of John, fulfilling the prophecy of Isaiah:

"A voice crying aloud in the wilderness,
'prepare a way for the Lord;
clear a straight path for him.
Every ravine shall be filled in,
and every mountain and hill leveled;
the corners shall be straightened
and the rugged ways made smooth;
and all mankind shall see God's deliverance'" (Luke 3:4–6).

In the prophetic tradition, John the Baptist warned of
God's judgment on the injustice of society. He also condemned the "establishment"; when he saw many of the
Pharisees and Sadducees coming for baptism, he said to
them: "You vipers' brood! Who warned you to escape from

the coming retribution? Then prove your repentance by the fruit it bears" (Matt. 3:7–8).

His message continued: "Already the axe is laid to the roots of the trees, and every tree that fails to produce good fruit is cut down and thrown on the fire" (Luke 3:8–9).

Luke reports Christ opened his ministry by reading in the synagogue from Isaiah:

"The Spirit of the Lord is upon me because he has anointed me;
he has sent me to announce good news to the poor,
to proclaim release for prisoners and recovery of sight for the blind;
to let the broken victims go free,
to proclaim the year of the Lord's favor."
He rolled up the scroll, gave it back to the attendant, and sat down; and all eyes in the synagogue were fixed on him.
He began to speak: "Today," he said, "in your very hearing this text has come true" (Luke 4:18–21).

In his message and ministry Christ proclaimed the coming of the Kingdom of God. This meant a radically new order of affairs, marked by repentance and a change of heart from within, and the creation of new ways for relating and serving corporately, in society. All this constituted a new "Kingdom," which had a spiritual reality, but which would begin to take concrete shape and form within society. Those who followed Christ were called to him and to this Kingdom of God as their first allegiance and loyalty. The existence of those committed to building this Kingdom and living according to the way of its Lord threatened the political order because it questioned the fundamental assumptions of established power and authority.

The Kingdom of God, though, was not to be identified with the seizing of political power, and it was not to be ushered in through any form of supposedly righteous violence and war. Here is where Christ parted company with the Zealots. Their messianic expectations, and those of many Israelites, visualized a politically triumphant Messiah who would be led by the power of the Lord to drive out the

oppressive Romans and establish God's Kingdom as a nationalistic theocracy ruling over them. But Christ's proclamation of the Kingdom of God was far more radical; it came
only through acts of unconditional, self-giving love—love
that reached even to one's enemies, and that called for ultimate surrender of the self for others.

The week between Palm Sunday and Good Friday presented Christ with the final temptation, in my view, to adopt
the Zealot's path of violent resistance. All through these days
the clash between Christ and the powers of society—the
coalition of Pharisees, Sadducees, Roman rulers and collaborators—became increasingly intense. They plotted for
a way to put Christ to death, as he fully knew.

After the Last Supper, when Jesus went to the Garden to
pray through the night, was he not tempted again by Satan,
who offered him the glories of a political kingship and power,
just as he had done earlier in the desert, if Christ would
contradict his message of love, and seize power violently?
The people had already been proclaiming him King and
Messiah; now, even in the Garden, some of his disciples had
taken swords and seemed prepared to fight. Certainly, these
must have been elements of the struggle and drama which
unfolded during that evening.[2]

But Christ would not betray his calling to do his Father's
will. "Not my will, but thine be done," was his prayer. True
messiahship, as foretold by the prophets, was found in one
who took the form of a Suffering Servant. That is how God
would accomplish his work of redemption, and call forth
a people who would be signs of a new order, of God's rule
over all.

So in the Garden, Christ gave himself over into the hands
of sinful men. At first some disciples resisted violently, only
to receive Christ's reprimand, "All those who take up the
sword shall perish by the sword" (Matt. 26:52). Then the
disciples fled in disarray and confusion; a few hours later
they denied that they ever knew him.

Many believe Christ was simply the victim of a miscar-
riage of justice, as if after doing miraculous deeds of mercy
and compassion he was suddenly seized without reason and

sent to his death. There is no question in my mind that the crucifixion of Christ was providentially destined as the means for humankind's salvation. As Isaiah foretold, "By his stripes we are healed." But we make a great mistake if we fail to see why this One, perfect in love, was condemned to death in his society, and who the people were who successfully conspired to send him to the cross.

Death by crucifixion was a Roman means for execution. Zealots and revolutionaries commonly died in that fashion. The Jewish method of execution for religious offenses such as blasphemy was stoning. Also, Pilate agreed to hold Jesus and instead free Barabbas; his crime, as recorded in Mark 15:7, was being one of the revolutionaries who had committed murder in a recent uprising. To the eyes of the Romans, the trade must have appeared reasonable.

Pilate could not find a conclusive case against Jesus. But the charge pressed against him by religious-political leaders was that he claimed to be "King of the Jews." As they reminded Pilate, "Any man who claims to be a king is defying Caesar" (John 19:12). When Pilate put that charge to Christ, he did not deny it, but at the same time, he made clear that his Kingdom was not simply a political one, such as that sought after by the Zealots. Pilate did not understand; but he did see clearly enough that the man standing before him, who had gained such a wide following among the masses and earned the animosity of the political-religious establishment, was a threat to the order of that society.

Luke writes that when the "elders of the nation, chief priests, and doctors of the law" assembled in their council to consider the case of Jesus (Luke 22:66–71), they asked him if he claimed to be the Messiah, the Son of God. With Christ's acknowledgment, they then took him to Pilate: "They opened the case against him by saying, 'We found this man subverting our nation, opposing the payment of taxes to Caesar, and claiming to be Messiah, a king' " (Luke 23:2). They added: "His teaching is causing disaffection among the people all through Judea" (Luke 23:5).

Ironically and pointedly, when Pilate sent Jesus to Herod, who questioned him and returned him to Pilate, Luke tells us, "That same day Herod and Pilate became friends; till then there had been a standing feud between them" (Luke 23:12). Two governing rulers, normally distrustful of each other, were united by their common fear of one who radically called into question their pretensions of power and authority.

Pilate consented to have "their king" crucified, obviously seizing the opportunity to underscore the establishment's loyalty to Rome. The shout by the crowd, "We have no king but Caesar" (John 19:15), must have made the Romans and all their collaborators euphoric.

Roman law required that the nature of the crime of one being crucified be written and attached to the cross where he hung. The accusation written by Pilate made plain the political nature of Christ's offense as seen through the eyes of the rulers: "Pilate wrote an inscription to be fastened to the cross; it read, 'Jesus of Nazareth King of the Jews'" (John 19:19).

We can understand the inherent tension between the Gospel of Jesus Christ and any existing political order by remembering that Christ was hung on a cross to die by the ruling powers of the State.

Chapter 5

Challenging the Powers

T HE REST OF the New Testament witness on this subject should be understood in light of Christ's resurrection, which proved his reign over all earthly powers and authorities. Paul writes in Ephesians 1:18–23:

> I pray that your inward eyes may be illumined, so that you may know what is the hope to which he calls you, what the wealth and glory of the share he offers you among his people in their heritage, and how vast the resources of his power open to us who trust in him. They are measured by his strength and the might which he exerted in Christ when he raised him from the dead, when he enthroned him at his right hand in the heavenly realms, far above all government and authority, all power and dominion, and any title of sovereignty that can be named, not only in this age but in the age to come. He put everything in subjection beneath his feet, and appointed him

as supreme head of the Church, which is his body and as such holds within it the fullness of him who himself receives the entire fullness of God.

Likewise, Paul tells the Colossians: "He disarmed the principalities and powers and made a public example of them, triumphing over them thereby" (Col. 2:15).

To understand the full impact of these truths, we need to grasp what Paul meant when he referred so frequently to the "powers" of the world. Basically, this refers to all those ideologies, forces, structures, and institutions that lie at the groundwork of a society or a culture, giving a sense of corporate cohesion. Biblical language and perspective see such "powers" as dominating human affairs and, in an invisible way, striving to determine human events in rebellion against God's sovereignty.[1]

Paul identifies the powers which rule over human life outside of Christ as the State (Rom. 13:1), customs and laws (Gal. 4:1–11), time and space (Rom. 8:38), life and death (Rom. 8:38), law and order (1 Cor. 2:8), philosophy and tradition (Col. 2:8, 14–16) and religions and ethical rules (Col. 2:20–22). When Paul wrote to the Christians at Colossae he addressed himself to the forces which were threatening to entice them away from Christ. The Colossian Christians, for instance, were struggling with the powers of human tradition and public opinion, with forces that would make them observe certain cultural, legalistic codes of behavior. "The 'world powers' under which mankind languishes, to which the Colossians risked falling subject once again, are definite religious and ethical rules, the solid structures within which the pagan and Jewish societies of the day lived and moved."[2] The point made by Paul is that by his cross Christ "has unmasked and disarmed the quasi-divine authority of these structures."[3]

In his letter to the Galatians, Paul also expresses himself as to the nature of the powers and their connections with the world and human events. "Now that you have come to know God, or rather to be known by God, how can you then turn again to the weak and beggarly world powers to whom

you want to be enslaved once more?" (Gal. 4:9). To seek
stability and purpose for one's life by giving divine sanction
to those worldly structures or "powers" is clearly irreconcilable with the claims of the Christian's new and greater Lord,
Jesus Christ. New life in him means a liberation from these
powers:

> . . . I am convinced that there is nothing in death or life, in
> the realm of spirits or superhuman powers, in the world as it
> is or the world as it shall be, in the forces of the universe, in
> heights or depths—nothing in all creation that can separate
> us from the love of God in Christ Jesus our Lord (Rom.
> 8:38–39).

However pointedly the Bible teaches us to see the powers
as slavery for the Christian, the fact remains that they are
still a part of God's fallen creation, holding life in line where
people do not know Christ's liberation. Thus in a world
alienated from God, the powers have a useful function: they
keep people alive and ordered in society. "The state, politics,
class, social struggle, national interest, public opinion, accepted morality, the ideas of decency, humanity, democracy
—these give unity and direction to thousands of lives. Yet
precisely by giving unity and direction they separate these
many lives from the true God; they let us believe that we
have found the meaning to existence, whereas they really
estrange us from true meaning." [4]

When Christ was crucified and rose from the dead, and
whenever the Gospel is proclaimed, the domination of the
world powers is put asunder. Previously these powers had
been "accepted as the most basic and ultimate realities, as
the gods of the world." [5] As we have seen, it was the powers
of established order, of governmental authority, of system-
atized religious piety, of pretentious law and rule who conspired to "do Christ in" and sent him to the Cross—in short,
the "powers of this age."

As the biblical scholar Hendrik Berkhof points out further
in his book *Christ and the Powers*, "The resurrection mani-
fests what was already accomplished on the cross: that in
Christ God has challenged the powers, has penetrated into

their territory, and has displayed that He is stronger than they." [6] This is the concrete meaning of the term *Lord*. The Old Testament knew that the Lord was the Master of History; the New Testament makes it more specific—it adds that Jesus Christ is Lord.

The victory of Christ, and his lordship over the powers, also means that in a fallen world awaiting its final redemption, the "powers" are ultimately used by a sovereign God for his purposes.

It is against this background that we must understand Paul's view of the State, as well as that in Revelation. The State is part of the "powers." The defeat of these powers, and their subjugation to the Lordship of Christ, is ultimately assured. Yet, that final victory will not be won until the end of time, with the Second Advent of Christ. Until that time, the world continues in rebellion and sin, while God's Kingdom takes partial root, built by and taking some shape among those who are called by Christ to his Body. In this situation, the State is given the limited, provisional, and temporary, but yet very crucial role of maintaining coherence in human society.

In New Testament perspective there are only two kinds of people, regenerate and unregenerate. Christ reigns over humanity's disobedience through the "powers," such as the State, side by side with the order of "redemption" where Christ rules in and through the obedience of his disciples. The State operates on principles which unregenerate man can understand and accept: power, coercion, violence. The New Testament accepts this condition of structured disobedience as necessary reality, but in no way gives divine sanction to all its actions. The orderliness in society sustained by the State is to insure that the Church can live and carry on her work. In this way, the State is God's servant, though the State does not realize nor accept this and must be continually reminded. Further, God's providence has designed it to function for the good of the people by establishing justice and restraining evil, a modest but essential role.

These principles are set forth in the New Testament passage most frequently turned to, and almost as frequently

interpreted out of context, in discussing the Christian's relationship to the State, namely, Romans 13:1–17. Those verses,
however, cannot be properly understood unless they are read
as one section of a coherent body of teaching on the subject
of love overcoming evil, which begins with Romans 12:17
and extends through Romans 13:10:

> Never pay back evil for evil. Let your aims be such as all
> men count honourable. If possible, so far as it lies with you,
> live at peace with all men. My dear friends, do not seek
> revenge, but leave a place for divine retribution; for there is
> a text which reads, "Justice is mine, says the Lord, I will re-
> pay." But there is another text: "If your enemy is hungry, feed
> him; if he is thirsty, give him a drink; by doing this you will
> heap live coals on his head." Do not let evil conquer you, but
> use good to defeat evil.
>
> Every person must submit to the supreme authorities. There
> is no authority but by act of God, and the existing authorities
> are instituted by him; consequently anyone who rebels against
> authority is resisting a divine institution, and those who so
> resist have themselves to thank for the punishment they will
> receive. For government, a terror to crime, has no terrors for
> good behaviour. You wish to have no fear of the authorities?
> Then continue to do right and you will have their approval,
> for they are God's agents working for your good. But if you
> are doing wrong, then you will have cause to fear them; it is
> not for nothing that they hold the power of the sword, for
> they are God's agents of punishment, for retribution on the
> offender. That is why you are obliged to submit. It is an
> obligation imposed not merely by fear of retribution but by
> conscience. That is also why you pay taxes. The authorities
> are in God's service and to these duties, they devote their ener-
> gies.
>
> Discharge your obligations to all men; pay tax and toll,
> reverence and respect, to those to whom they are due. Leave
> no claim outstanding against you, except that of mutual love.
> He who loves his neighbour has satisfied every claim of the law.
> For the commandments, "Thou shalt not commit adultery,
> thou shalt not kill, thou shalt not steal, thou shalt not covet,"
> and any other commandment there may be, are all summed
> up in the one rule, "Love your neighbour as yourself." Love

cannot wrong a neighbour; therefore the whole law is summed up in love.

The teaching of this Scripture is that for the Christian, love overcomes vengeance; evil is never to be repaid by evil, but overcome by good. The Christian is called to sacrificial, unconditional love of others, and that includes love of enemies. Further, the "law" that the Christian is to follow is summarized and satisfied wholly by love of God and of one's neighbor—love of all humanity. The final and uncompromised claim on the Christian's life, then, is the obligation of such love.

As Paul writes to the Christians in Rome, the capital of the empire, the question obviously occurs whether this same attitude applies to even those pagan rulers in power over them, such as Nero. Paul says that it does. Rulers, regardless of any apparent evil, are not exempt from this command of love.

Under such an ethic, is evil never to be punished? Does not justice include the notion that persons are to be held accountable before society for their actions, particularly actions which are harmful or destructive of others? Paul recognizes that there is such a need, and that civil government performs this task. Whether it does so fairly and justly, or abusively and oppressively, and what the consequences are, is a question not dealt with in this passage, but addressed elsewhere in the Bible. The point Paul makes is that seeking such justice in a world where sin still reigns is a legitimate function of the State. Insofar as that task involves repaying evil with some other form of evil, though, the Christian can have no part; his or her encounter with Christ reveals the universal truth that evil is never overcome with evil, but rather with love.

It is important to note that here Paul speaks idealistically about the responsibilities of the State and its intended purpose as a "servant of God." He does not address the truth made all too obvious in Paul's own life that the State, since it is also in rebellion, will commonly act in ways not in

keeping with its appointed end. Paul's frequent imprisonment by the State provides several cases in point.

Students of New Testament Greek who have the skills
of biblical exegesis point out a fascinating perspective on
the word used by Paul which we sometimes translate as
"obey" in this section of Romans. They say it does not mean
"obey" as we would typically understand it; three other
Greek words used in the New Testament have that meaning, but the one chosen here by Paul rather implies a re-
ciprocal obligation. In Ephesians 5:21, Paul uses the same
word in saying, "Be subject to one another out of reverence
for Christ." This does not mean an uncritical obedience to
an authority's every command, but rather, a spirit of mutual
reciprocity. The original Greek means then that the Christian
should be willing to recognize a legitimate sense of subjugation to earthly authority, just as the State is to be subject to
its limited purposes for humanity in God's ordering of all
creation. In the final end, and in the workings of God's
providence which naturally transcend our understanding,
the actions of the State, including its evil, are subjected to
God's rule over all history. In Christ, the ultimate power
of the State over humanity has been subdued and defeated.
He now reigns over all, and the Christian can live in that
reality.

The first verses in Romans 13 are frequently cited out of
their full context as proof that government is a divine institution, or that the authority of government should always
be unconditionally obeyed. The passage in its entirety, however, supports neither of these assertions. Theologians differ
on what this passage, and the teachings of the Bible, say
about the State. Some, especially Lutherans, have traditionally
claimed that whatever particular government exists is willed
by the providential action of God; thus, the shape of its life
is generally ordained and mandated by God. My own view
is that such a perspective is not sufficiently grounded in
Scripture, and in actual experience has fostered great naïveté
and unwarranted acceptance of the corporate sin of government. It is hard to believe that the government of Hitler's
Nazi Germany, for instance, was divinely instituted and

mandated, or that the same holds true for the autocracy of the Soviet Union. It is harder still to believe that God divinely institutes certain governments but not others.

Another view is that the principle of government is ordained as a necessary part of God's plan. That is different and far more helpful, I believe, for it recognizes that a particular government can fall far from carrying out the principles intended for government in general.

A third theological view maintains that the original Greek commonly translated as "ordained" in this passage should more properly be "ordered"—an important difference, for it implies that particular governments are simply utilized by God in his ordering of the entire cosmos. This view corresponds to Paul's assessment of the "powers" in the other passages we previously discussed. Those "powers," including the State, are in no way divinely instituted or ordained as institutions embodying God's will and authority. Quite the contrary, despite their rebellious and sinful nature, they are recognized and used by God, as Lord over all, in his providential ordering of a fallen creation. But they carry no absolute and final authority, by any means. Further, Christ has triumphed over these powers, and the Christian is thereby freed from their bondage as he is made new in Christ. The point of reference and authority for the Christian is always Jesus Christ as Lord.[7]

In this respect, there are similarities between Paul's frequent discussion of the Law and his treatment of government; both are a part of God's instituted order, but because of the action of Jesus Christ, neither can be considered as reliable or unquestioned depositories of divine authority. God's ordering, or even "ordaining," of these two realities in no way implies the Christian's uncritical obedience to them, as the other writings of Paul and the New Testament make clear.

I do not pretend, in any way, to be a theologian; yet it seems obvious to me that Christians who, on the basis of Romans 13, look to government as a divinely instituted source of God's authority are making a grave biblical mistake. misinterpreting Scripture and harming their Christian witness.

Rather, we must never lose sight of the responsibility to call government into judgment and account to see that it nurtures justice, as defined biblically. Also, as reflected in the more sound of the theological views just discussed, the Christian must always view government as part of a fallen order and as motivated by its own pretensions and striving for power. As such it must never be the final authority for the Christian; rather, the revelation of Jesus Christ, and his triumph and love, must be seen as the final judge and authority over all government.

The full thrust of Paul's teaching in Romans 12:17 to 13:10 is that the mandate of love transcends that of conditional obedience to other earthly authority; our unqualified obligation to love. How ironic it is that Christians have commonly used excerpts from this passage as proof of their obligation to cooperate with a government in acts of vengeance, injustice, oppression, violence, and war.

Romans 12–13 (and the similar passage in 1 Peter 2:13–17) in no way exhausts the New Testament's teaching on the State, a fact frequently overlooked by Christians. The life of the New Testament Church, as recorded in Acts, gives practical examples of how Christ's apostles and the State of their time interacted. In Acts 16, for instance, Paul claims his Roman citizenship as a means of demonstrating the injustice that has been done to him. He and Silas had been flogged and thrown into jail without any trial, contradicting their legal rights. It can be said Paul was witnessing to the State by demonstrating the failure of its purported standards of justice, and insisting on a redress of this grievance. In the words of one teacher of the New Testament, giving honor to authorities does not "forbid one to claim whatever legal rights one has over against the government. Paul was not showing disrespect for the magistrates at Philippi, but was rather paying them true respect, when he insisted on his legal rights and thereby summoned them to a proper sense of their own dignity." [8] As Bob Sabath of the *Post-American* writes, "Submitting to the authorities does not mean submitting to their illegal acts." [9]

In Thessalonica, Paul had a similar experience (Acts 17). Opponents of the Gospel seized Jason in their futile search for Paul and Silas, and came before the magistrates saying, "The men who have made trouble all over the world have now come here; and Jason has harboured them. They all flout the Emperor's laws, and assert that there is a rival king, Jesus" (Acts 17:6–7). New Testament scholar F. F. Bruce has pointed out that when Paul writes back to the Christians at Thessalonica and tells them that "we were exceedingly anxious to see you again . . . but Satan thwarted us" (1 Thess. 2:18), he was probably referring to the repressive action of State's authorities.[10] Also, the complaint made about anti-Roman actions was much like the charges brought before Paul and Silas in the previous incident at Philippi: "These men are causing a disturbance in our city; they are Jews; they are advocating customs which it is illegal for us Romans to adopt and follow" (Acts 16:20–21).

Earlier in Acts, in a dramatic account, Peter and the apostles, while preaching and teaching fearlessly in Jerusalem, were brought before the Sanhedrin, "the full Senate of the Israelite nation" (5:21). This body was the center of civil and criminal authority.

> So they brought them and stood them before the Council; and the High Priest began his examination. "We expressly ordered you," he said, "to desist from teaching in that name; and what has happened? You have filled Jerusalem with your teaching, and you are trying to make us responsible for that man's death." Peter replied for himself and the apostles: "We must obey God rather than men. The God of our fathers raised up Jesus whom you had done to death by hanging him on a gibbet. He it is whom God has exalted with his own right hand as leader and saviour, to grant Israel repentance and forgiveness of sins. And we are witnesses to all this, and so is the Holy Spirit given by God to those who are obedient to him" (Acts 5:27–32).

What was at stake here was not merely the right of the apostles to preach the Gospel, but the fact that in their preaching and their teaching, the authority of the established order in society was undermined and judged. It was that order who crucified Jesus; but God had now made him Leader, Lord, King, and Savior, so that Israel corporately could repent and turn from her wicked ways. The issue at hand, then, was the recognition by the State of the radical implications of this Gospel, calling into judgment its pretensions of power and authority, which prompted the State's attempted repression.

The Church can never make a true peace with the State and still preserve the wholeness of the Gospel by promising to leave politics alone and speak only about faith. Proclaiming the whole Gospel of Jesus Christ as Lord has inherent political consequences, as the early Church quickly discovered.

When Paul wrote Romans 13 in about A.D. 57, the Roman Empire and Nero had not yet begun their serious persecution of the Church. That was unleashed a few years later, in A.D. 64. Even so, Paul had referred to the authorities as acting as instruments of Satan after his experience in Thessalonica, as we have seen. This theme of the demonic character of the State emerged with force during the history of the early Church and the writing of the New Testament. We find its culmination in the Book of Revelation, where the State is pictured as the "beast from the abyss," possessing the full powers of Satan and doing his work in the world.

> Then out of the sea I saw a beast rising. It had ten horns and seven heads. On its horns were ten diadems, and on each head a blasphemous name. The beast I saw was like a leopard, but its feet were like a bear's and its mouth like a lion's mouth. The dragon conferred upon it his power and rule, and great authority. One of its heads appeared to have received a deathblow; but the mortal wound was healed. The whole world went after the beast in wondering admiration. Men worshipped the dragon because he had conferred his authority upon the beast; they worshipped the beast also, and chanted, "Who is like the Beast? Who can fight against it?"
> The beast was allowed to mouth bombast and blasphemy,

and was given the right to reign for forty-two months. It
opened its mouth in blasphemy against God, reviling his
name and his heavenly dwelling. It was also allowed to wage
war on God's people and to defeat them, and was granted authority over every tribe and people, language and nation. All
on earth will worship it, except those whose names the Lamb
that was slain keeps in his roll of the living, written there since
the world was made.

Hear, you who have ears to hear! Whoever is to be made
prisoner, a prisoner he shall be. Whoever takes the sword to
kill, by the sword he is bound to be killed. This is where the
fortitude and faithfulness of God's people have their place
(Rev. 13:1–10).

This description, about the same State Paul referred to in
Romans 13, was probably written a mere thirty-five years
later, near the end of Domitian's reign in A.D. 90–95. Some
commentators reason that the seven heads of the beast, which
are later explained as seven kings in Revelation 17:10, are
actually the seven emperors from Caesar to Domitian. That
would indicate the consistent satanic power which had expressed itself through the reign of that empire, from the
time of Christ to when Revelation was written. In any event,
the message is clear: the Roman Empire served as the instrument of Satan.

It cannot be argued that this description of the State is
limited to the Roman Empire of that time, any more than
Paul's words in Romans 13 apply only to that empire.
Rather, Revelation completes the biblical understanding of
the State, and is applicable throughout history. Thus, the
beast in Revelation symbolizes the demonic element, with
its potential for ascendancy, in any and all worldly power.
Should that picture seem startling and hard to accept, let us
remember the temptations of Christ in the desert. Satan's
offer to give to Christ the kingdoms of the world in exchange
for his worship of Satan implies that they were in Satan's
power to give over. Yet we know that Christ triumphed over
Satan, and over the powers of this world, with his redeeming death and resurrection. So the final demise of such

satanic power is certain, but it is only completed at the end
of time. Revelation 18 gives us a picture of this defeat and
the triumph of Christ:

> After this I saw another angel coming down from heaven;
> he came with great authority and the earth was lit up with
> his splendour. Then in a mighty voice he proclaimed, "Fallen,
> fallen is Babylon the great! She has become a dwelling
> for demons, a haunt for every unclean spirit, for every vile and
> loathsome bird. For all nations have drunk deep of the fierce
> wine of her fornication; the kings of the earth have committed
> fornication with her, and merchants the world over have grown
> rich on her bloated wealth."
>
> Then I heard another voice from heaven that said: "Come
> out of her, my people, lest you take part in her sins and share
> in her plagues. For her sins are piled high as heaven, and God
> has not forgotten her crimes. Pay her back in her own coin,
> repay her twice over for her deeds! Double for her the strength
> of the potion she mixed! Mete out grief and torment to match
> her voluptuous pomp! She says in her heart, 'I am a queen on
> my throne! No mourning for me, no widow's weeds!' Because
> of this her plagues shall strike her in a single day—pestilence,
> bereavement, famine, and burning—for mighty is the Lord
> God who has pronounced her doom!"
>
> The kings of the earth who committed fornication with her
> and wallowed in her luxury will weep and wail over her, as
> they see the smoke of her conflagration. They will stand at a
> distance, for horror at her torment, and will say, "Alas, alas
> for the great city, the mighty city of Babylon! In a single hour
> your doom has struck!"
>
> The merchants of the earth also will weep and mourn for
> her, because no one any longer buys their cargoes, cargoes of
> gold and silver, jewels and pearls, cloths of purple and scarlet,
> silks and fine linens; all kinds of scented woods, ivories, and
> every sort of thing made of costly woods, bronze, iron, or mar-
> ble; cinnamon and spice, incense, perfumes and frankincense;
> wine, oil, flour and wheat, sheep and cattle, horses, chariots,
> slaves, and the lives of men. "The fruit you longed for," they
> will say, "is gone from you; all the glitter and the glamour are
> lost, never to be yours again!" The traders in all these wares,
> who gained their wealth from her, will stand at a distance for
> horror at her torment, weeping and mourning and saying,

"Alas, alas for the great city, that was clothed in fine linen and purple and scarlet, bedizened with gold and jewels and pearls! Alas that in one hour so much wealth should be laid waste!"

Then all the sea-captains and voyagers, the sailors and those who traded by sea, stood at a distance and cried out as they saw the smoke of her conflagration: "Was there ever a city like the great city?" They threw dust on their heads, weeping and mourning and saying, "Alas, alas for the great city, where all who had ships at sea grew rich on her wealth! Alas that in a single hour she should be laid waste!"

But let heaven exult over her; exult, apostles and prophets and people of God; for in the judgement against her he has vindicated your cause!

Then a mighty angel took up a stone like a great millstone and hurled it into the sea and said, "Thus shall Babylon, the great city, be sent hurtling down, never to be seen again! No more shall the sound of harpers and minstrels, of flute-players and trumpeters, be heard in you; no more shall craftsmen of any trade be found in you; no more shall the sound of the mill be heard in you; no more shall the light of the lamp be seen in you; no more shall the voice of the bride and bridegroom be heard in you! Your traders were once the merchant princes of the world, and with your sorcery you deceived all the nations."

For the blood of the prophets and of God's people was found in her, the blood of all who had been done to death on earth (Rev. 18:1–24).

The power, the pretension, the vainglory, the corporate sins of exploitation and rapacious luxury stand for Babylon of old, for the Roman Empire of that time, and, we must say, even for America.

Every State has within it a demonic potential, the New Testament tells us. Further, it suggests that the nearly unavoidable temptation is for Caesar to claim that which is God's, and thereby become the instrument of Satan. Every State, pluralistic and totalitarian, faces this temptation in the glorification of its mission, its righteousness, its authority, its divine blessing, its power, and its nationalism.

Yet the State is a part of God's order. It is intended to function, in a fallen world where evil reigns, as a servant of God. But this role is only temporary and provisional and is always in danger of becoming an instrument of demonic power. We can live, however, in the hope of knowing that Christ is Lord over all.

On the basis of the material we have briefly examined, I think we can summarize certain basic biblical principles which should guide the Christian in his or her relationship to any State. First, there is the clear scriptured admonition, mentioned often, to pray for those in authority. Such prayer, in my view, should recognize that the rulers of this world find themselves faced, usually unconsciously, with the temptations of power resulting from the spiritual warfare raging in the world. I know such talk sounds foreign and strange to our modern, secular culture; yet, I am convinced that such biblical insight has a deep relevance to this era. Those in positions of authority need our prayers not only for wisdom in facing difficult decisions, but also so that the State may resist those cunning and persistently powerful temptations which would make it an instrument of evil, rather than let it seek its intended and humble place in the divine order of things.

With prayer goes a certain respect for those holding authority, mentioned by Paul and similarly by Peter (1 Pet. 2:17). This respect, however, is rooted in the proper and intended mandate that should be sought by those who hold earthly authority. Often, the Christian may see this mandate far more clearly than the one in authority, and hold it up with greater seriousness. Such respect in no way prohibits criticism and rebuking of those individuals in their misuse of authority. John the Baptist and Christ, as well as the prophets, give us clear examples.

Then, the Christian is to obey the laws of government, so long as this does not entail any disobedience of Christ, the Lord and King.

The principle of paying taxes is clearly accepted by the New Testament, for the government has valid and important functions to perform. However, whether specific portions of tax might be withheld from the government for activities which the Christian cannot condone could still be an open question not totally answered from Scripture; either side of

such an argument could offer strong points from the Bible
and Church history.

Next, the Christian is called to responsible disobedience
of the government if and when obedience would entail disobeying God, a principle set forth clearly by both teaching
and example in the Bible. However, the Christian is still
personally accountable for such actions and must willingly
suffer the consequences inflicted by the State. This part of
the Christian's witness is evidence of faith in the Lordship
of Christ, and for the glory of the Lord.

Finally, and most importantly, the Christian community,
by its very being, is called to witness to the State with
prophetic power. From the Old Testament through the New,
we see that God, speaking first through the prophets and
then in Jesus Christ, rules over history as Lord, speaking
his Word to the world. That Word shatters the myths and
pretensions of earthly power, calling them to repentance,
and holding forth the understanding of their true identity.
This is how the Word addresses us today, in our individual
hearts and in the corporate world. As we proclaim and embody its life, we inevitably witness to earthly authority—to
the State. That Word may not be heard; or it may be heard,
undermined and rejected, and even persecuted. Christ warned
his disciples:

> "You will be handed over to the courts. You will be flogged
> in synagogues. You will be summoned to appear before gov-
> ernors and kings on my account to testify in their presence.
> But before the end the Gospel must be proclaimed to all na-
> tions. So when you are arrested and taken away, do not worry
> beforehand about what you will say, but when the time comes
> say whatever is given you to say, for it is not you who will be
> speaking, but the Holy Spirit" (Mark 13:9–11).

The personal consequences of our allegiance to Christ will
differ with the specific nation and historical time in which
we find ourselves. But our task remains the same: to witness
to the Good News of Jesus Christ, and to build his new
society, his Kingdom, which takes root within his Body,
the community of believers. Membership in that Body will

invariably place the believer in tension with manifestations of earthly power, which make constant but fraudulent claims on the Christian's loyalty and faith. Every State, in some way, will do so. Yet we know that Christ is building his Kingdom, that we are called to be a part of it, and that in this new order, all history finds its true meaning and fulfillment.

It is not unusual, then, that we should live as a "pilgrim people," as if we are foreigners in this land, without our true and ultimate allegiance given to another Kingdom, in obedience to its sovereign Lord.

As a "peculiar people" called by God, Christians may find that the State is so threatened by their existence that brutal persecution results. If so, we may be called to suffer and even die, always returning hatred with love, always leaving vengeance to the Lord. In other cases, the State may be more tolerant. Then the Church faces temptations of another kind, for she will find the State trying to seduce her into legitimizing and blessing its existence and its actions. The natural tendency of any State is toward idolatry and self-glorification. Believing that a State has a special calling in history, or a particular mandate of God, or embodies the hope for humankind's future all evidence the subtle power of such idolatry. The task of the Church in that case is to preach the Word, resisting all the idolatry claimed by the State, and to live out in its witness the Church's identity as first fruits of God's new creation. That never comes through accommodation to the values of a fallen world, but rather through living as "faultless children of God in a warped and crooked generation in which you shine like stars in a dark world and proffer the word of life" (Phil. 2:15–16).

John Howard Yoder provides a succinct summary of the relationship of Christians to any State when he writes: "No State can be so low on the scale of relative justice that the duty of the Christian is no longer to be subject; no State can rise so high on the scale that Christians are not called to some sort of suffering because of their refusal to agree with its self-glorification and the resultant injustices." [11]

Chapter 6

The
Constantinian
Legacy

W HY HAS THE biblical witness of the Christian's relationship to the State become so distorted? What has been the record of those who call themselves Christians throughout history? Why have Christians become so accustomed to believing that their faith requires allegiance to the existing order, rather than commitment to another Kingdom? These were my questions as I began to consider the areas of civil disobedience, nonviolence, and participation in war in connection with the case of Smitty Flynn. More generally, they were questions which increasing numbers of thoughtful people were raising with urgency during the days of our intense involvement in Indochina.

As I dug into the early history of Church-State relations, I began to see how and why the Christians of the first three centuries had a dramatically different relationship to governing

authority from that of Christians in our own time and culture. More importantly, I also began to discover what caused
the Church to abandon these earlier perspectives and become
a part of the political "establishment." All this provides insight and guidance for re-establishing in our own day a
Church that is marked by biblical authenticity and power in
its witness to our culture.

As an important part of the background of the early
Church's relationship to the State, we need to recognize the
role of authority the Roman Empire assumed in the lives of
its citizens. During this period the State attempted to control
its people's religious convictions by requiring citizens of the
Roman Empire to bow down before the Emperor as well as
before the pagan gods. The pluralistic religious beliefs within
a State, which we usually find in modern democracies, did not
exist. (Some historians, however, have noted that the Roman
Empire did tolerate a variety of different religions throughout their domain.) The early Church soon found that allegiance to the State at certain points could be diametrically
opposed to the commandments of Christ. Thus, at major and
direct points of conflict, the Christians as a body put their
lives in danger in resistance to civil commands.

According to the records of history, three concrete points
in the early Church's understanding of the Gospel brought
Christians into direct disobedience and conflict with existing
Roman law. These examples only characterized the broader
attitudes held by the early Church toward the secular culture
and government of that era. First of all, Christians, because
of their commitment to making Christ Lord over all, could
not under any circumstances give allegiance to, or repeat
any oath in support of, the Emperor and the Roman Empire.
Second, this commitment caused Christians to refuse legal
obligations to serve on court juries or for the most part to
participate in the legal and political structures of that day.
Third, these early Christians refused induction into the Roman Army. In other areas, however, historians indicate that
in general the Church did obey the State authorities. Its
members paid their taxes, and even further, they were noted
for paying them consistently and without fail.

During this early period the Christian community lived in strong and real awareness that they were set apart, and that there was a great need to prepare for the return of Jesus. Christians saw themselves as a Kingdom within the Roman kingdom and consequently felt little loyalty to the State, other than indifferent obedience to it at points where it did not conflict with their relationship to God. According to G. J. Heering, an authority on early Church history, "there was lack of any strong sense of adhesion to the State in which the Christian lives, a lack of national consciousness. In a world which, to their way of thinking, was alien, often hostile, they felt themselves to be already citizens of the Eternal Realm for which they waited." [1] This strong sense of citizenship and loyalty to God obviously left no room for unconditional loyalty elsewhere. Perhaps in no other time since then have Christians been so unified as a body of believers, accepting the claims and commands of Jesus as well as living according to the reality of the promised Kingdom of God.

Regarding the refusal of Christians to give an oath or a "sacrifice" to the state, we must remember that the Empire required unconditional allegiance to the Emperor and the pagan gods. The noted Church historian Cecil J. Cadoux states the situation quite clearly:

> It was in the abstract perfectly possible for the pagan law at sundry points to contravene the law of Christ. In actual practice, the only case that occurred regularly was the State's demand for sacrifice to the pagan gods and to the Emperor. The exact legal status of Christians in the Empire during this period has been the subject of much discussion: but broadly speaking, they were technically liable at any moment to be required to sacrifice to the pagan gods, and sentenced to death if they refused. While the matter was one of police administration, and no law specifically directed against the Christians appeared yet to have existed, the requirement of sacrifice was always represented as the Emperor's command.[2]

Two points seem clear from the early historical sources. First, the Christians did not go out of their way to boast of their nonallegiance to the Emperor, whose laws they felt were transcended by the laws of God. Rather, Christians tended to live at peace with the State until the State forced them to make a commitment in opposition to their faith— a commitment the Christians refused to make. Second, this act of sacrifice to show allegiance required by Roman law was not created primarily to antagonize Christians and to bring conflict to a head; rather, it was simply an act occasionally required by the State to assure loyalty among all its citizens, not an uncommon requirement for any state. Thus, the early Church resisted the normal attempts of the Empire to ask for the allegiance of its citizens. Christians also refused to use the court systems and were critically detached from the political and legal structures. One basis for this stance was the conviction that the State's laws were inconsistent and unjust. Tatianus, an early Christian scholar, said of the Roman law, "I condemn your legislation, for there ought to be one common government for all, but now there are as many codes of law as there are states, so that things that are disgraceful among some are honorable among others." [3] After commending the unity and wholeness of God's law as presented through Hebrew scripture, he further stated, "If human laws are thus mutually inconsistent, it follows that at least some of them must be wrong." [4]

The Christians' own principles required them to abstain from all retaliation or reprisal or even resistance in case of wrongdoing. As Cadoux points out, to injuries which they could not avert by love, gentleness and conciliation, they submitted and even suffered:

> This meant, not only that they could not take on the office of judge or executioner, but that they could not appeal to the law-courts for the redress of injuries. The motives that ordinarily prompt men to prosecute, the considerations that a judge regards as compelling him to pass sentence—had no weight with them. . . . It will suffice here to mention a couple of passages from the apology of Athenagoras, which make it clear that the Christians of his day regarded the Sermon on the Mount as forbidding litigation. He speaks of Christians as "having learned not only not to hit the striker back, and not to go to law with those who plunder and rob us, but to some,

if they buffet [us] on the side of the head, to turn the other side of the head for a blow, and to others, if they take away [our] tunic, to give [our] cloak as well." They "display good deeds, [namely], not hitting back when they are struck, and not going to law when they are robbed, giving to those that ask, and loving their neighbors as themselves." He speaks of it as a well-known fact that Christians could not endure to see a man put to death.[5]

These same general views caused early Christians to look with suspicion and disapproval on positions of political power. Many Church Fathers maintained outright that a Christian could not hold public office because of the obvious contradictions that would be imposed upon his faith. One of them, Tertullianus, argued that the insignia of political power and the accompanying forms of dignity were idolatrous, and quite unlike the example set by Jesus who rejected the seeking of public power and acclaim. Tertullianus argued that a Christian might hold office if it involved no taking of an oath, no judgment of capital or criminal charges, no pronouncements of penalties, and no infliction of bondage, imprisonment, or torture on anyone [6]—a striking picture of the inherent conflicts for the Christian who evaluated the exercising of secular political power. Early Christians regularly questioned and condemned the motives of pride, wealth, lust for power, and perpetuation of injustice which characterized the lives and actions of those who possessed political power.

The attitude of the early Church toward the State caused the Roman official Celsus to write a noted discourse in about A.D. 178, urging Christians to undertake the duties and responsibilities of government, and to participate within the legal system. He argued that if all citizens acted as Christians did, the Empire could not be maintained. This sort of argument, of course, held no reason nor power for the Christians.

The principle of nonparticipation in the Roman legal system, then, was simply an evidence and outgrowth of the broader view of Roman political authority. One writer, impressed that these Christians were so dedicated in obedience to God and his law as over and above the legal structures

and obligations of their time, declared "The Christians sur-
pass the laws by their own lives." [7] It is also interesting to
note that Paul advises the Corinthian Christians in 1 Corin-
thians 6 not to bring their suits and legal matters before the
State's courts, but to avoid them.

Lastly, we must consider the refusal of early Christians to
obey induction orders into the army of the Roman
Empire. Several actual cases are recorded. Eusebius, a fourth-
century historian, tells us of a young man of twenty-one from
Numidia named Maxmilian who appeared before the African
proconsul, Dion, for induction into the army. Maxmilian
refused induction, stating simply, "I cannot serve for I am a
Christian." Dion replied, "Get into the service or it will cost
you your life." Maxmilian's last remark was, "I do this age
no war-service but I do war-service for my God." [8] He was
executed March 12, A.D. 295, and his father, also a Christian,
returned home in pride of his son's unbending loyalty to
God. Cadoux reports that there were many cases like this
which may have led to the massive persecution of Christians
in A.D. 303. This type of commitment was indicative of the
seriousness to which the early Christians took the commands
of Christ relating to fighting, war, and bloodshed. Justinus,
an early Christian apologist, wrote, "We, who hated one another, and slew one another on account of differing customs,
now since the coming of Christ, become sociable, and pray
for our enemies, and try to persuade those who hate us un-
justly, so that they, living according to the fair precepts of
Christ, may share our same hope of receiving the same reward from the God who rules all things." [9]

Certain features of Roman military life raised a specific
ethical conflict for Christians: (1) the extensive shedding of
blood on the battlefield; (2) the fact that military officers
took judicial power into their own hands to pass death sentences on criminals, and common soldiers were asked to execute these sentences; (3) the use of torture, scourging and
crucifixion in handling prisoners; (4) an oath of unconditional loyalty to the military system; (5) the inhuman behavior of soldiers in peacetime among the civilians of states
under the occupation of the Empire.[10]

These factors, taken together, constituted a powerful deterrent against military service for any Christian. He took too seriously the commands of Christ to accept a life-style encompassing actions contrary to those commands.

The Roman official Celsus, who was keenly aware of the nonresistance position of the Christians, continually insisted that they fulfill their duty to the State. Again, he stated that if everybody followed the ethic of nonresistance the Empire would be ruined. Origen, a learned Church Father in the third century, rebutted the position of Celsus as follows,

We have come in accordance with the counsel of Jesus to cut down our arrogant swords of argument into plowshares, and we convert into sickles the spears we formerly used in fighting. For we no longer take swords against a nation, nor do we learn anymore to make war, having become sons of peace for the sake of Jesus, who is our Lord.[11]

Yet, as Bainton, a foremost historian of the early Christian Church has stated, the Christians were not working in these matters to overthrow the Empire. "A reason more definitely assignable for their unwillingness to take up arms was their certainty of vindication in the life to come. The primary grounds of their aversion was the conviction of its incompatibility with love." [12]

The quality of love set forth by Jesus, and later by Paul, had not been lost in the early Church. "If we are to love our enemies," Tertullian, a third-century Christian Father, asked, "whom have we to hate? Who then can suffer injury at our hands?" [13]

This brief survey of Christian civil disobedience in the second and third centuries provides ample evidence, I believe, that Christians justified their position according to what we would consider today very literal and fundamental acceptance of the written Scripture. They simply believed the claims and commands of Jesus and strove to live by God's just and complete law of love.

I want to stress that this sketch of the relationship of the early Church to the Roman Empire before the rule of Constantine is intended largely to give a feeling for the mind-set of these early Christians. In no way am I an authority in the history of this period; but I have tried to fairly summarize what scholars have written about the early Church of this time.

Two other factors are important in the comparison between the situation of the early Church and today. It is clear that *some* civil disobedience by Christians came as a result of the "religious" claims made by the Empire. Yet, other cases of disobedience (such as the Christians' unwillingness to submit to the legal system and their refusal to be inducted into the army) did not stem directly from the Empire's religious pretensions, but rather from the injustice that Christians saw in civil institutions when contrasted with the demands of Christ. Despite the differences between their relationship to the Empire and our own pluralistic society, the parallel to our own time seems clear.

Second, although the separation of Church and State firmly engrained within our system insures the freedom of worship, we must still ask: does our "secular" state continue to make religious claims on its citizens? We have freedom of religion; yet we do not always have freedom to decide when one can or cannot kill another for the protection of the State. We do not have freedom to decide whether we shall personally help finance an army that is spread throughout the world in part to protect an economic empire. These and similar examples certainly may involve one's religious convictions. Yet, with certain exceptions, a decision not to give the State final allegiance here may result in prosecution. Even the secular State, or a "pluralistic" society, can make claims on its citizens similar to those made by a Caesar who sets himself up as a god.

The stance of the early Church toward the Roman Empire, and the pretensions of power inherent within that Empire, resulted in the frequent persecution and martyrdom of Christians. Popularized versions of hymn-singing Christians thrown to the lions may have distorted for us the situation of those first believers. Their persecution was not simply a result of a mad tyranny; the Roman Empire was lauded as the zenith of civilization, and looked to as a legal and political model, in contrast to the barbarians outside its borders as well as to the so-called "Dark Ages" which followed the Empire's collapse. Rather, the plight of these Christians and the severity of their persecution was due in large measure to their uncompromising obedience to Christ and his Kingdom, which made them a disconcerting thorn in the side of the political establishment. Following the Way of their Lord, their full commitment to a life of self-giving love, and their belief in a New Order of life for humanity, which they proclaimed and lived, threatened the security and power of the mighty Roman Empire.

The annals of the persecution suffered by the early Church frequently record believers declaring in court before their judges, "I am a Christian," as the simple response to charges and the answer to questions. On many occasions, fellow Christians in the courtroom would rise up courageously proclaiming their protest against the unjust sentencing of believers, thereby revealing their own identity as Christians and then receiving the death sentence themselves.[14]

With the coming to power of Constantine in A.D. 312, such persecution ceased, and ensuing events dramatically changed the relationship of the Christian Church to the State. The consequences of Constantine's conversion shaped the Church's attitude toward the State for the next fifteen hundred years, building up a legacy which has been with us to the present, distorting Christians' understanding of Scripture even in our own time.

Unlike Maxentius, his chief political rival for power over the Empire, Constantine was not in sympathy with the popular religion of his culture. He could not appeal to the regular deities of society for support. Despite their persecution, Christians had grown in strength and significance throughout the Empire. So as he led his forces against Maxentius, Constantine decided he would appeal to the Christian God, and thereby His followers, for support. When, in the confrontations which followed, he was successful, he could then say that this God must have put him in power.

The circumstances surrounding Constantine's so-called

conversion have been widely discussed by historians. It is hard to escape the conclusion that a good measure of opportunism was involved; the support of Christians was essential to the coalition of political power devised by Constantine.

To ensure the Church's support and active cooperation in upholding the Empire, Constantine radically changed the State's stance toward Christians, making an offer which the Church, regrettably, could not refuse:

1. Church clergy were exempted from taxes and from military duty.
2. The Church was allowed to set up a court system of its own, so Christians would not have to take part in imperial courts, and a Roman citizen could be tried in either.
3. Church authorities were given the privilege of owning and receiving property.[15]

Such measures were designed not simply as favors from a sympathetic ruler, but as a means for gaining a measure of control over the Church, and for redirecting the loyalty of its members to the Empire. Constantine knew that the loyalty and support of Christians could only be gained by acknowledging their faith. A unified empire, internally at peace, was possible only if the troublesome resistance of the Christians to Roman authority and power could be overcome. Constantine's appeal for the support of the Church became a means for establishing significant control over its life. As one historian puts it, "From Constantine's time matters of Christian doctrine and discipline were affairs of State." [16]

One can set forth the rationalizations which led the Church Fathers into an almost blind embracing of the Empire. After all, years of harsh persecution had suddenly been halted, and the Emperor had declared his belief in the God of Christianity. Was this not the work of God? Might it not signify, in some measure, a new age, even as pretold by Scripture? Did not the Pax Romana which reigned through the "civilized world" serve as a further sign that the Empire was now ordained and sanctified by God?

History gives us the advantage of seeing the utter fallacy in those perspectives. It is one thing for Christians to rejoice when the State ceases outright persecution; but it is quite another thing to respond to a policy of religious tolerance by granting the Church's spiritual blessing and religious support to the reigning political establishment. Whenever the Church pays such a high premium for assuring its acceptance by society and guaranteeing its institutional security from secular authority, it tends to distort the biblical understanding of the Church's relationship to the world and its powers.

The Empire itself was not transformed by the reported conversion of its Emperor. It was not suddenly committed to seek the justice taught by Christ, but still sought the ends of its own self-preservation and prestige, frequently at a bloody cost. In no way had the Roman Empire suddenly become a "Christian" Empire, molded by the teachings of Christ or committed to judging or fashioning itself according to the qualities of biblical justice. This is worth remembering today whenever we are tempted to suppose that the path to establishing self-righteousness for a nation lies simply through electing a committed Christian as President, or encouraging our leaders to pray and share a personal faith.

The change in the Empire that came with Constantine's rise to power was purely external so far as Christian faith was concerned. But the change in the Church was dramatic, far-reaching, and eventually disastrous. As the Empire secured the Church's countenance and blessing, Constantine lost no time in enlisting Christians as a bulwark of support for the power of an unregenerate political and social order. The willing collaboration of the Church which began then, distorted its witness to the world for ages that followed.

The most immediate and probably most dramatic change came in the attitude of Christians toward serving in the Roman army. Since it was through soldiers, and with the blessing of the Christian God, that Constantine won his confrontation for power, he naturally declared that his legions should honor that God. Following his orders, thousands of soldiers came into the Church, often only as a public gesture so as not to jeopardize their position in the army. The

Church, which now was rapidly becoming totally indebted to Constantine for its security and protection, commended the practice of "converting" the armies. Totally reversing its previous history of widespread pacifism and noninvolvement in the army, the Church urged Christians in the Roman legions to remain there, and then, in A.D. 314, threatened excommunication to Christians who "throw away their weapons in time of peace." [17] Christian soldiers were now viewed as good soldiers, protecting a "Christian" State against a "heathen" world. The uncompromising apostles of peace who characterized the Church of the second and third centuries now were replaced with crusaders for the Empire; those who had fought in spiritual warfare for the sake of Christ now suddenly had become the soldiers of Caesar.

> At the Council of Arles, the Church not only condemned the constant practice of Christian soldiers hitherto of bidding farewell to the ensign of war, but even put it under the fearful ban of excommunication. Thus it is proclaimed in the name of the Church that the military authority has gained full support from the new concord between State and Emperor on the one hand and Christianity and the Church on the other. By this decision the Church completely revised her attitude to the army and war, the attitude that has prevailed until now, at least in theory. The Church had longed to win the Emperor, and now flung herself into his arms.[18]

Such a drastic change in the Church's posture took place over time. Naturally this new stance had to be rationalized, but the reasons did not always come easily. One Church Father, Athanasius, declared: "Murder is not permitted, but to kill one's adversary in war is both lawful and praiseworthy." [19]

In the first or second century of its life, a Church less weary from harsh persecution, and a Church closer in history and in spirit to the life of its Lord and his apostles might well have recognized the perversion of discipleship which came in reaction to Constantine's opportunistic overtures. But at this critical juncture of history, a Church now entering its fourth century found active collaboration with the

power structure of the Empire a temptation it could not resist. It chose to collaborate in a way which compromised and
nearly obliterated certain clear commands of its Lord. By
the fifth century the transition was culminated, as the army
became restricted to *only* those who were "Christians."

Augustine struggled hardest in the years after Constantine
to reconcile the witness of Christ to this collaboration with
earthly imperial power. In dealing specifically with the question of violence and war, he constructed the "just war"
theory which held, basically, that Christians should fight in
wars which were "good" or justifiable. His criteria can be
summarized as follows:

1. War is permissible only after all other efforts have
   failed.
2. The intention of the war must be good—for example,
   defense against attack.
3. Noncombatant immunity must be preserved—no burning, massacres, or killing of innocent.
4. The force used in war must be proportionate to, and
   in keeping with the goals sought. This force is subject
   to change constantly depending on changes of intention or goals.
5. The defect of any of these conditions would make any
   war wrong.[20]

Like others, Augustine saw the Empire as the protector of
Christianity, and argued that Christians should protect the
Empire. So the cause of war became righteous. Despite his
attempt to apply ethical discrimination to the problem of
war, the effect, both then and later, was to suggest that the
State could feel justified by the Church in making war. As
a case in point, Augustine assumed that the cause of Rome
was just, and that of the barbarians unjust. History rarely
sustains such simplistic views of good and evil. The barbarians who invaded the Empire had constantly been pushed
out of their lands, and 30,000 were eventually slaughtered
by Roman soldiers. Augustine's conviction that "The Roman
Soldiers are in the service of justice and peace"[21] was the

tragic consequence of his strenuous efforts to rationalize the Church's underwriting of the Empire and its political order. Parallels in history abound, as the State increasingly looked to the Church to justify its warring pursuits.

The Church's alliance with the Empire had consequences far beyond reversing the early Christians' tradition of not participating in war; this was only one manifestation of a basic overall change in the Church's relationship to existing political power. Other important consequences also need to be remembered.

Not the least of these was a secularization of the Gospel, for the distinction between the Christian community and the world began to be seriously blurred. Christianity was made into an "official religion," and as a result, many of the cultural mores of the time, including those of pagan faiths, infiltrated Christian practices. In addition, the State encouraged the Church to organize itself bureaucratically, thus making it easier for the State to exercise its power and influence within the Church. As the Church evolved more and more into an institutionalized organization, its concerns about its own security threatened to eclipse the vitality of its faith and witness. Small committed bands of believers who nurtured their fervent faith and fellowship in the catacombs of Rome now were replaced by a Church organized by an official centralized bureaucracy.

Once the first steps of this wedlock between Church and State were taken, it was only a matter of time before it came to fruition in religious wars and crusades, which killed thousands in the name of Christianity. The bond grew stronger through promulgation of such doctrines as the divine right of kings. Not until the Reformation was this existing synthesis of political and spiritual power questioned. Even then, what emerged was a compromise belief that rebellion led by some in political authority against unjust and tyrannical superiors might be justifiable. The voices of others raised more fundamental questions about the Christian's relationship to political power, be it tyrannical or revolutionary, but they remained a minority within the Reformation movement.

Because of the Constantinian legacy, contemporary Christians tend to derive an understanding of their relationship to the State from culture and history far more than from Scripture. It is no wonder that many Christians are in the habit of quoting selectively, and out of context, Paul's words in Romans 13 as the Bible's definitive teaching about politics; the Church has been doing this ever since the fourth century when it rationalized its embrace of Constantine. But as we free ourselves from the prejudices of tradition, nationalism, and culture, and look to the Scriptures and to the lives of those first believers who strove to live in faithfulness to their Savior, we can discover anew what it means for the Body of believers today to live with an uncompromised allegiance to our Lord.

Perhaps the agony of Vietnam and Watergate will aid us in rediscovering the inherent tension between our faith and the pretensions of the State. Like the Church in the fourth century, we have opted largely for a "Constantinian alliance" in seeking to confer divine blessing and sanction on America and her undertakings. Thus, multitudes of Christians—especially evangelicals, with a strong commitment to Scripture—persisted in believing that Vietnam was a righteous crusade rather than a national sin. Most of those same believers clung to a faith in the Presidency, rather than believe the biblical truth that the pretensions of power and pride will ultimately entrap and destroy those who attempt to rule with "kingly" authority.

Recovering a biblical perspective of political power can guide our lives and shape the community of God's people into a dramatic witness to the Kingdom of our Lord. We can begin to taste its life now. Living as a Body of believers in faithfulness to him, we can embody a radical alternative to the beliefs and values clung to by the secular world, and thereby hold forth a vision of hope. Moreover, we will then come to regard the actions of those like Smitty Flynn not as questionable or irresponsible, but rather as understandable expressions of uncompromised allegiance to Christ and his Kingdom.

Chapter 7

Civil Religion
and Biblical Faith

JOHN STENNIS, the Senator from Mississippi, called to ask if I would be willing to speak briefly to the 1973 National Prayer Breakfast on behalf of the Senate prayer breakfast group. The year before, John said, Senator Strom Thurmond had been given this task; he is at the opposite end of the political spectrum, so now I was being asked in order to maintain a "balance." I told John I would consider prayerfully his invitation.

I had serious reservations. They sprang from my concern over ways in which events like Presidential prayer breakfasts can deeply confuse the biblical relationship between the political order and the Church. The Constantinian legacy continues to be with us, subtly sanctifying the status quo.

The more I observe contemporary America while reading the Scriptures and the history of the Church, the more I sense how dangerous it is to mix our piety with patriotism. The Christian, like every citizen, cannot avoid being "political"; our values, attitudes, life-style, and actions or inactions all have concrete political ramifications. I believe we as Christians must recognize this reality and make a determined effort to bring the political side of our lives under the authority of Jesus Christ. Our politics must never be ruled by thoughtless conformity to the secular culture.

Our culture is not Christian in the truest sense of the word: as a culture, we do not accept the ultimate authority of Jesus Christ over all people and nations. We do not all believe that our ultimate trust must be placed on God's work of salvation and redemption. Yet American culture is "religious" in superficial ways. "In God We Trust" is engraved on our coins. Nearly every President of the United States has made public references to God or Divine Providence, although few have referred to Jesus Christ. Most Americans think that religion is important in giving their nation strength and success. As President Eisenhower said: "Our government makes no sense unless it is founded in a deeply felt religious faith, and I don't care what it is."

"Civil religion" is the term commonly used to refer to these generally shallow public expressions of religious values. Included are the notions that God has blessed and chosen America as he did Israel and that George Washington was like Moses leading the people out of bondage into a new land. It suggests that the Constitution and the Declaration of Independence were composed after inspired prayer meetings.

We must distinguish between civil religion and biblical faith. It is true that many of the first settlers came to America with a deep sense of religious mission and a vision of a new order for the glory of God. Documents like the *Mayflower Compact* attest to a strong heritage of spiritual ideals and sentiments. Yet, civil religion distorts the relationship between the State and our faith. It enshrines our political order, and fails to speak of repentance, salvation, and God's standard of justice. The promised land becomes a nearly perfect land, and we are given a sense of righteous mission to the world. America's actions become spiritually ordained.

Even in war we are beyond reproach, for we are fulfilling some sort of divine destiny. American civil religion wanted us to believe there was honor in the "peace" we claimed to have won in Vietnam (before the victory of the opposing side in 1975), and that the war could be vindicated as necessary and right.

My worry was that the National Prayer Breakfast could serve as another vehicle for enshrining the civil religion of our nation. As I thought about the major events of the past years, including the Vietnam War and the related policies carried out by national administrations, and then recalled the wholehearted support they received from millions of Christians across the land, I was dismayed. Wouldn't a prayer breakfast like this be seen as giving God's blessing to these policies? Yet I felt an obligation to those in the Senate prayer breakfast group who had made the request; further, many of those in the prayer breakfast movement have been my closest friends—like true brothers to me. I understand the vision of their mission, and I know what has happened in the lives of many throughout the nation who have committed themselves to meet weekly in small, unpretentious prayer breakfast groups.

Some of my most trusted associates thought that I should quietly decline John Stennis' invitation. But that seemed cowardly. He had asked me to share whatever was on my heart. If I had reservations about this National Prayer Breakfast, and if I felt the need for a spirit of repentance among the people of the land, why shouldn't I share those thoughts openly? I called my longtime friend Doug Coe, who has given himself for years to the prayer breakfast movement, and told him of my feelings. Doug said I should simply say whatever the Holy Spirit seemed to direct me to share. I called John back and told him I would accept the invitation.

The nation had recently completed the 1972 Presidential election campaign, and a "cease-fire" of sorts had been proclaimed in Vietnam. It was called a "peace with honor." There was an overpowering impulse in America to believe that we had done no wrong—that we could come out of Indochina "holding our heads up high." This same spirit of haughty pride was echoed in the Administration at that time. Hints and charges of potential corruption in the campaign, including the Watergate matter, were arrogantly dismissed as being unfounded or even slanderous. The country was clinging to an image of national self-righteousness, and doing so precisely at the time when we most needed to look carefully at our sins.

I wrestled with what I should say, and consulted with several friends, asking them for suggestions. Then, the morning before the event, I took a close associate from the office, went down to the cafeteria for a cup of coffee, and there put together from various drafts the final version of my remarks.

The people coming to the National Prayer Breakfast—over three thousand in number—would be the leaders of government, industry, and education; many of them were wealthy and powerful and were attending the breakfast primarily because the President as well as other national leaders would be present. Others were attending out of deeper conviction and faith. My intention was to say some word which would be relevant to them, and faithful to my own convictions; to give a faithful witness to truth and to my Lord. My own honest thought, however, was that my comments would go largely unnoticed by all but a few.

It was not until I arrived at the Washington Hilton that morning, and took my seat at the head table, that I began to sense the tension growing inside of me. My longtime friend Billy Graham was seated next to me on my left; President Nixon was to my right. Cabinet officers and other members of Congress were all nearby. I could not help but think, am I going to make a fool of myself before all these friends and associates? It was that feeling we all know which bids us to go along with the crowd, or not to risk doing something that may displease people whose friendship we deeply value. Those thoughts and feelings flashed through me.

Once I began my comments, however, I felt comfortable and at peace. As I was talking I vividly remember looking out into the audience and seeing frowning, hostile looks on the faces of Bob Haldeman and John Ehrlichman, seated directly in front. What I said now seems relatively general and inoffensive; yet it expressed the concerns on my heart:

My brothers and sisters:

As we gather at this prayer breakfast let us beware of the real danger of misplaced allegiance, if not outright idolatry, to the extent we fail to distinguish between the god of an American civil religion and the God who reveals Himself in the Holy Scriptures and in Jesus Christ.

If we as leaders appeal to the god of civil religion, our faith is in a small and exclusive deity, a loyal spiritual Advisor to power and prestige, a Defender of only the American nation, the object of a national folk religion devoid of moral content. But if we pray to the Biblical God of justice and righteousness, we fall under God's judgment for calling upon His name, but failing to obey His commands.

Our Lord Jesus Christ confronts false petitioners who disobey the Word of God: "Why do you call me 'Lord, Lord' and do not the things I say?" (Luke 6:46).

God tells us that acceptable worship and obedience are expressed by specific acts of love and justice: "Is not this what I require of you . . . to loose the fetters of injustice . . . to snap every yoke and set free those who have been crushed? Is it not sharing your food with the hungry, taking the homeless poor into your house, clothing the naked when you meet them, and never evading a duty to your kinsfolk?" (Isa. 58:6–7).

We sit here today, as the wealthy and the powerful. But let us not forget that those who follow Christ will more often find themselves not with comfortable majorities, but with miserable minorities.

Today, our prayers must begin with repentance. Individually, we must seek forgiveness for the exile of love from our hearts. And corporately as a people, we must turn in repentance from the sin that scarred our national soul.

"If my people . . . shall humble themselves, and pray, and seek my face, and turn from their wicked ways, . . . then I will forgive their sins, and will heal their land" (2 Chron. 7:14).

We need a "confessing church"—a body of people who confess Jesus as Lord and are prepared to live by their confession.

Lives lived under the Lordship of Jesus Christ at this point in our history may well put us at odds with values of our society, abuses of political power, and cultural conformity of our church. We need those who seek to honor the claims of their discipleship—those who live in active obedience to the call ". . . do not be conformed to this world, but be transformed by the renewing of your minds" (Rom. 12:2). We must continually be transformed by Jesus Christ and take His commands seriously. Let us be Christ's messengers of reconciliation and peace, giving our lives over to the power of His love. Then we can soothe the wounds of war, and renew the face of the earth and all mankind.

I sat down, glad everything was over. The rest of the breakfast continued. The President drew strong applause when he said, "For the first time in ten years at one of these breakfasts the President of the United States is able to say that the United States is at peace in Vietnam." The Paris "Peace Accords" had been signed just a few days earlier.

Leaving the breakfast I noticed that some of the President's associates were unusually cool toward Antoinette and me. Back in my office that afternoon, I was besieged by telephone calls. Some came from members of the press, wanting to know why I said what I did; others came from members of Congress and of the Executive Branch who privately indicated their warm support of my comments. Several others, including a Cabinet member, sent personal letters to the same effect.

It was not until later, however, that I learned what had transpired at the White House. People there were infuriated. They regarded my remarks as a personal attack on the President. At the White House press briefing that day, they had considered having Ron Ziegler express their offense at the impropriety of my remarks, but that was dismissed on the ground that it would only increase attention to what I had said. Subsequently, I learned that rumors were being spread to discredit me. It was evident that a response of harsh vindictiveness was coming from the White House. I was dismayed, but tried to restrain my feelings of resentment and bitterness. It seemed to be a clear case of loving my enemies; this was confirmed later in the year, when I learned that I was in fact on the White House "enemies" list.

Press accounts the next day drew the conflict more fully into the public eye. The CBS Evening News broadcast the day of the breakfast featured portions of my remarks contrasted to the President's, and the *New York Times* ran the following story:

Nixon Hears War Called a 'Sin'

By JAMES T. WOOTEN

Special to the New York Times

WASHINGTON, Feb. 1—President Nixon, the Rev. Billy Graham and three Russian atheists were among the more than 3,000 people who attended the 21st National Prayer Breakfast here today and heard a long-time foe of the Vietnam war call it "a sin that has scarred the national soul."

With the President and his wife sitting inches away, Senator Mark O. Hatfield, the Oregon Republican who consistently opposed Mr. Nixon's military policies in Southeast Asia, told the audience of Government leaders and their friends and families that they should seek individual and collective forgiveness for the country's role in the hostilities there.

"Then," he said, "we can soothe the wounds of war and renew the face of the earth and all mankind."

His comments were part of a 90-minute program of prayers, Biblical readings and remarks from members of Congress, the Supreme Court and the President in an annual religious gathering of Government leaders in the International Ballroom of the Washington Hilton Hotel.

The breakfast, begun in 1953 as an expansion of smaller but similar programs in both the Senate and the House, have traditionally been nonpartisan and passive.

Nevertheless, after more than a week of what were described as "struggles between propriety and conscience," Senator Hatfield, wearing a green blazer, strode to the lectern and, without mentioning the war, mourned its existence as a fact in American history and asked his listeners to regard it as an "exile of love from our hearts."

His words fell on the ears of many of the most vigorous supporters of the country's participation in the war—hawkish Congressmen, Air Force and Army generals, Navy admirals —but their applause when he concluded his remarks was both sustained and energetic.

The President, whose comments were the final words of the breakfast, did not allude to Senator Hatfield's remarks but focused rather on the events of his fourth year in office—his trips to the People's Republic of China and the Soviet Union, and the final resolution of the Paris peace negotiations before his closing paraphrase of an old religious song.

"Let there be peace on earth," the President said, "and let it begin with each and every one of us in his own heart."

The recently signed peace agreement and the ceasefire in Vietnam were also the central themes in the prayers and brief speeches from Mrs. Ann Armstrong, a special counsel to the President; Representative John T. Myers, the Indiana Republican; Harry A. Blackmun, an Associate Justice of the Supreme Court, Representative Carl Albert, Speaker of the House; James E. Johnson, an Assistant Secretary of the Navy, and Arthur F. Burns, chairman of the Federal Reserve Board.

Each of them spoke of the relationship between religion and the nation's future. Directly in front of the lectern from which they spoke sat Anatoly F. Dobrynin, the Ambassador from the Soviet Union, and Vladimir Promysolv, the Mayor of Moscow, and his wife.

The three Russians are all members of the Communist party, for which a prerequisite is a declaration of atheism.

The Mayor and his wife are touring Washington this week, and all three Russians were invited to attend the breakfast by its planners.

Representative Albert H. Quie, Republican of Minnesota, presided at the breakfast in the absence of Senator John C. Stennis. The Mississippi Democrat was shot twice Tuesday night in a robbery in front of his Washington home and is in serious condition at Walter Reed Army Medical Center.

In his opening remarks, Representative Quie, sweeping his arm across the audience of Government officials and staff members, said, "We see ourselves as a gathering of sinners."

That brought slight titters from some quarters of the spacious ballroom before he introduced Senator Hatfield, a devout Baptist and a long-time member of the Senate prayer group that meets regularly on Wednesday mornings.

Several days before he was shot, Senator Stennis, the leader of the Senate group, asked Senator Hatfield to speak at the breakfast, and the Oregon legislator replied that he was reluctant because he would feel compelled to speak his mind.

Senator Stennis, according to Senator Hatfield, said he should have no hesitation to say precisely what he believed.

"But needless to say, I wrestled with it," the Senator said after the breakfast. "I finally decided that so often these public religious exercises take on the essence of pageantry rather than substance, and I just couldn't be part of that."

Such services as the prayer breakfast "seem to be using God and what should be a deeply spiritual experience to merely create some surface justification for policies that have already been enacted," the Senator said.

"My point is that while we may represent power," he concluded, "we are not omnipotent."

The Senator is of the same religious faith as Mr. Graham, who sat next to him at the breakfast and pronounced the benediction for the program by asking divine assistance and guidance for the President "when he returns to the Oval Office."

I had made no direct mention of the Vietnam war, nor of the President. The intent of what I had to say was directed toward the corporate national spirit of self-righteousness; certainly this was epitomized by the War and the lack of any penitent response among millions of Americans. The President fully shared and embodied that spirit, so it is understandable that media would draw to the surface the contrast between that sentiment and what I had said. Yet interpreting the incident as a direct confrontation with the President overlooked the deeper thrust of the remarks, and intensified the tension between Nixon loyalists and me.

In the days that followed there was an amazing response from Christian publications and groups throughout the country. From the *Christian Century* to prominent evangelical periodicals there were requests to reprint the statement, and editorial statements of support. Likewise, mail flowed into the office that was, for the most part, tremendously supportive of what I had said. All this amazed me. I had never expected that my comments would either receive much notice or stimulate the encouraging response from nearly every quarter of the Church.

Not all agreed fully with my remarks, however, and some who did not were among my most respected Christian friends. Billy Graham thoughtfully and prayerfully set forth his own reactions by letter (reproduced here with Dr. Graham's permission):

February 9, 1973

Senator Mark Hatfield
Senate Office Building
Washington, D.C. 20500

My dear Mark:

I personally appreciated your boldness in using the name of our Lord Jesus Christ at the Prayer Breakfast last Thursday. In recent years I have felt the program perhaps unwittingly was moving toward the more unitarian form of civil religion which is legitimate in state functions and has been used since Washington's day. However, I think your talk was used to remind us of the original concept of these breakfasts and that they were from the beginning "Christian." . . . But I noted with deep concern that the press interpreted your remarks as political and as a rebuke to the President! I am sure you would agree with me that the National Prayer Breakfast should never be used to air political views and differences. It would quickly destroy the non-political idea behind the Breakfast, and perhaps discourage future Presidents from participating. It seems to me that the Breakfast should be a time of praying for and encouraging our political leaders—especially the President!

If I had any suggestion to make it would have been that you as a war critic could have turned to the President and commended him for his determination and perseverance in getting the cease-fire in Vietnam. This would have had a unifying effect that the Country desperately needs at this time.

As you already know I have an affection for President Nixon as a man and as a personal friend. I believe him to be one of the most sincere, dedicated and able men ever to occupy The White House. He has shaken history as no other President

since Roosevelt. He has set an example in self-discipline,
family life, church attendance, et cetera, that is helping the
Country through a great spiritual crisis—and despite differences in certain political areas he deserves to be commended
especially by Christians.
God bless you always.

                                        Billy Graham

President Nixon had just achieved what appeared to many
as a peace in Vietnam. He had overwhelmingly won re-
election three months earlier, and was just entering his second
term with enthusiastic, deep support throughout the nation.
His foreign policy initiatives the previous year to Peking and
the Soviet Union seemed as creative, hopeful steps. The
corruption which would later destroy him was then being
successfully and completely covered up from us all. In that
context, then, Billy was forcefully and honestly sharing
understandable personal convictions which I took deeply
to heart.

I have always held Billy in the highest esteem as a faithful
friend. Our relationship goes back to the 1950s, when I was
serving as Secretary of State in Oregon, just beginning my
political career, and Billy was conducting his famous New
York Crusade in Madison Square Garden. When visiting
New York I went to the crusade one night, and then to the
concluding rally in Times Square. These times were pivotal
experiences in revitalizing my personal Christian faith. More
than the crusades themselves, however, was the opportunity
to become personally acquainted with Billy during that week.
We met privately together, discussing issues of faith and
beginning a deep relationship that was to continue to grow
over the coming years. So naturally, Billy's letter to me was
troubling. In replying, I suggested that we spend some time
together to talk about some of these issues. Later we found
the opportunity to do so.

I was deeply concerned, frankly, that Billy was running
the risk of being "used" by the White House. I did not deny
his call to be in a pastoral relationship with Presidents. But
being a true pastor to one in power, in my view, also had to

involve an awareness of how any political authorities tend to seek blessing from the Church for their policies. Thus, the Christian must maintain the duality of a pastoral and prophetic witness toward the powerful; indeed, I believe this duality is necessary in all the mission of the Church. The concern on my heart was that Billy's genuine pastoral care for the President might be causing him to overlook how people in the Administration could be tempted to exploit that relationship to their own ends.

As I shared my concerns with Billy, and he further explained his own perspectives, we were able to minister to each other. Our views evolved and shifted as we continued to seek each other's counsel on future occasions. Through all that has happened in the years since then, we have grown in our understanding of our witness to the world, and in our relationship to each other.

Many believe that civil religion is better than no religion at all. But I wonder. Civil religion, in my view, is not a harmless, generalized unitarianlike depository of belief, which can help people reflect upon God, or even provide helpful ethical guides for the country. Rather, because most civil religion is devoid of both the prophetic dimension of biblical faith and of the centrality of God's revelation in Jesus Christ, it becomes highly vulnerable to being exploited as a tool of national self-righteousness and even idolatry. History has shown that a little bit of religion, taken out of context, often does more harm than good. Christians who hold to the integrity of their faith should insist on its wholistic application, and resist piecemeal versions as unbiblical. That principle should guide our perspectives on civil religion.

Warning against the dangers of civil religion must not be taken as advocating that the affairs of state be kept totally insulated from the truths of Christianity. On the contrary, we bring the political realm into an authentic relationship of judgment and dialogue with biblical faith. That necessitates beginning with a faith that is neither truncated nor enculturated, but whole, grounded in God's revelation.

Are there examples from history which might point more insightfully to mature interaction of religious faith and political responsibility? I think so. One that has intrigued me was demonstrated by Abraham Lincoln.

A couple of years ago I began reading Elton Trueblood's *Abraham Lincoln, Theologian of American Anguish.* Dr. Trueblood mentions Lincoln's action on a number of occasions to proclaim special days of humiliation, fasting and prayer. I was especially attracted to the wording of such a proclamation issued on April 30, 1863. This was during the very depths of the Civil War, three months after he had issued the Emancipation Proclamation and three months before the Battle of Gettysburg. The political turmoil of 1973 and 1974 echoed in some ways the crisis a century earlier, and there were parallels in the nation's unrest and introspection. You can readily see the relevance of Lincoln's words from these excerpts:

> Whereas it is the duty of nations as well as of men to own their dependence upon the overruling power of God, to confess their sins and transgressions in humble sorrow, yet with assured hope that genuine repentance will lead to mercy and pardon, and to recognize the sublime truth, announced in the Holy Scriptures and proven by all history, that those nations only are blessed whose God is the Lord; . . .
>
> We have been the recipients of the choicest bounties of Heaven; we have been preserved these many years in peace and prosperity; we have grown in numbers, wealth, and power as no other nation has ever grown. But we have forgotten God. We have forgotten the gracious hand which preserved us in peace and multiplied and enriched and strengthened us, and we have vainly imagined, in the deceitfulness of our hearts, that all these blessings were produced by some superior wisdom and virtue of our own. Intoxicated with unbroken success, we have become too self-sufficient to feel the necessity of redeeming and preserving grace, too proud to pray to the God that made us.
>
> It behooves us, then, to humble ourselves before the offended Power, to confess our national sins, and to pray for clemency and forgiveness.

Naturally, because of my convictions about the grave dangers of civil religion, I questioned whether this was simply another example of mixing piety with nationalism. The answer was found in the wording of Lincoln's proclamations. His was not a spirit of shallow patriotism and glorification of the State, but a realistic and humble confession of the political system's failure to measure up to God's standards of righteousness and justice. Lincoln had a profound awareness of the sovereignty of God and the shortcomings of the nation.

Lincoln offered an alternative to the pious patriotism of civil religion. His call for prayer and fasting was not in a spirit of national self-righteousness but of genuine repentance. He believed that only through the acknowledgment of our corporate guilt and confession of national sins could the country regain its national purpose and unity. He did not ask for allegiance to any sect or denomination. He did not have in mind that the State establish a Church. His plea was for examining the nation's failures against the uncompromised standards of God's justice.

On a number of occasions in 1973, I concluded speeches and articles by citing Lincoln's proclamation of 1863. Those who heard and read it responded enthusiastically. They were stirred by its relevance during a year of despair over a war which continued in spite of a "peace with honor," a political scandal unfolding in Washington, and rumblings of global economic difficulties. In the course of the year, suggestions were made to me that Lincoln's proclamation be modified and proposed to the Congress for adoption, and then issuance by the President.

December 20, 1973, was not an ideal time to present a new resolution in the Senate. The city of Washington was still shovelling its sidewalks after a heavy snowstorm. Congress was pushing toward the Christmas recess, attempting to complete action on a number of major bills, including a new national speed limit and appropriations for defense and foreign aid. Nevertheless, I decided to introduce such a resolution, hoping a Senate committee could approve it, have it pass the Senate, and then sent to the House for concurrence before its observance on April 30, 1974, coinciding with the date of Lincoln's 1863 proclamation.

Only a few Senators were on hand on the morning of December 20th when I had been given permission to present my remarks in support of Senate Joint Resolution 183, to proclaim April 30, 1974, as a National Day of Humiliation, Fasting and Prayer.

In introducing the resolution I made the following observations:

> We are all troubled by the continual erosion of the American people's faith and trust in their leadership in all parts of life. The current fuel shortage has caused us to reevaluate the legitimacy of our excessive use of the world's natural resources. We witness a country torn apart with division and lacking the spiritual foundation that would restore its vision and purpose. We, as a people, through our own acquiescence to corruption and waste, have helped to create a moral abyss that produces a disdain for honesty and humility in high levels of national leadership. . . .
>
> There is hope for a land and a people who have the capacity to recognize their sins and their faults, and turn from them. Repentance means precisely this—to turn the other way. In so doing, we recognize that past events and present conditions cannot be rationalized or justified; rather, they must be repented of, so a whole new way can be sought. This is how individuals and how our land as a whole can seek authentic renewal and transformation. So it is with this hope that I commend to the Senate this resolution calling for a Day of Humiliation, Fasting and Prayer in our land.

Drafting the resolution I kept the relevant sections from Lincoln's 1863 proclamation and added a part referring more directly to the failings of the twentieth century:

> Whereas, we have made such an idol out of our pursuit of "national security" that we have forgotten that only God can be the ultimate guardian of our true livelihood and safety; and
>
> Whereas, we have failed to respond, personally and collectively, with sacrifice and uncompromised commitment to the unmet needs of our fellow man, both at home and abroad; as a people, we have become so absorbed with the selfish pursuits of pleasure and profit that we have blinded ourselves

to God's standard of justice and righteousness for this society; and

Whereas, it therefore behooves us to humble ourselves before Almighty God, to confess our national sins, and to pray for clemency and forgiveness: Now, therefore be it resolved by the Senate and House of Representatives of the United States of America in Congress Assembled, that the Congress hereby proclaims that April 30, 1974, be a National Day of Humiliation, Fasting and Prayer; and calls upon the people of our nation to humble ourselves as we see fit, before our Creator to acknowledge our final dependence upon Him and to repent of our national sins.

I realized that passage of the resolution depended to a great extent on the reaction of the Democratic leadership, and that the ultimate impact of the proposal depended on the inner response of millions of Americans. Exercising his judgment as Majority Leader, Senator Mike Mansfield offered to allow immediate consideration of the resolution, rather than have it referred to a committee.

Its surprisingly quick passage in the Senate, followed by the addition of numerous cosponsors, did not result in similar action in the House of Representatives. There, the resolution was sent to the House Judiciary Committee, where it remained buried under other business. Appeals made by some to the President to issue the proclamation on his own authority brought the response that the President customarily took such action only at the direction of Congress. Actually, it had been done both ways in the past.

The impact of the resolution was not destroyed by the failure of the House to act, however. By April 30, 1974, thousands cooperated fully with the spirit of the resolution, abstaining from food, suspending normal activities, and reflecting on our national shortcomings.

It is difficult to measure the effects of a special observance such as this. Although it came and went unnoticed by some, for others as well as myself it was a deeply moving experience. On the Senate floor there was a two-hour "colloquy," or series of speeches centered on the theme of the resolution, led by Harold Hughes, then Senator from Iowa. The press headlined Senator Barry Goldwater's questions about the use of the word, "humiliation," which he found offensive. What I had hoped to convey by using Lincoln's word "humiliation" was a deep concern for our undeniable national failings. There were many who would have preferred to have this sentiment watered down, but I felt it was at the heart of the whole issue.

For my own part, I had decided to clear my schedule that day for meditation and prayer with my family. Eventually, however, I accepted Dr. Louis Evans' request that I take part in a service at the National Presbyterian Church in Washington, D.C. A portion of the liturgy led by Dr. Evans conveys the spirit of the service:

Leader: O God, your justice is like rock, and your mercy like pure flowing water. Judge and forgive us. If we have turned from you, return us to your way; for without you we are lost people. From brassy patriotism and a blind trust in power, deliver us, O God.

People: From public deceptions that weaken trust; from self-seeking in high political places, deliver us, O God.

Leader: From divisions among us of class or race; from wealth that we will not share, and poverty that feeds on food of bitterness, deliver us, O God.

People: From neglecting rights; from overlooking the hurt, the imprisoned, and the needy among us, deliver us, O God.

From every part of the country came reports of gatherings large and small, in observance of this day. For some, it was the first experience of fasting and an excellent preparation for understanding the increasingly severe problem of hunger in the world. The response came from cities as large as Dallas, Texas, where the participation was very extensive, and from much smaller places like Fossil, Oregon, with a population of a few hundred. Warm words of appreciation came from people in other countries as well, such as Sweden, El Salvador and Ghana.

It would have been surprising if there had been no opposition to the Day of Humiliation, Fasting and Prayer. In addition to the questions raised on the Senate floor, there were others who objected to the observance. One lady in Oregon wrote, "Pray for the nation's sins—indeed! . . . The only sin I feel is having you represent Oregon." Another indignantly asserted, "I think it's a little presumptuous of you and your congressional cohorts to declare April 30 a religious day. . . . Will you propose a day for atheistic rejoicing?" A resident of the state of Washington wrote to the editor of the *Portland Oregonian,* "I personally am tired of pompous self-righteous people assuming they have the right to say what sins our country is guilty of. We must overcome the unhealthy mental attitude of guilt and go on with the business of living in this world for better or for worse. Instead of humiliation, let us have a National Day of Pride in Being an American."

As we celebrate our Bicentennial, the dangers of the Church misusing civil religion and confusing the clear Word of biblical faith will be accentuated. Our temptation is to believe that the spiritual motivations evident in many of America's early settlers can be appropriated today to give the nation an aura of divine sanction and blessing. That is precisely the kind of national idolatry which the Scripture, as we have seen, so forthrightly speaks against. America's destiny will only be jeopardized by attempts to assure ourselves of a special spiritual preference. Presenting to the nation the claims of God's justice and his compassion for all people is a legitimate and urgently needed task for the Church. Perhaps appeals to past idealistic rhetoric and religious vision set forth by earlier Americans can be helpful. But telling America, and ourselves, that she is a nation with a distinctive spirituality, or a special relationship with God, is a betrayal of the biblical witness. The Church must have no part in that kind of a message.

Much of the organized Church today, in my opinion, has allowed its thinking and its values to be conformed to the world. In subtle ways we have succumbed to a civil religion instead of obeying the Scriptures and the revelation of Christ.

We must rediscover the relevance of Jesus' words as we live forth our witness, and challenge the values of our culture. "Do not be conformed to this world," Paul tells us. As the Phillips translation puts it so vividly, "Don't let the world around you squeeze you into its own mold, but let God remold your minds from within, so that you may prove in practice that the plan of God for you is good, meets all his demands, and moves toward the goal of true maturity" (Rom. 12:2). How difficult it is today to avoid the temptation of conformity to twentieth-century American culture. But a Church which is the captive of a political system or a message that merely echoes the values of secular society cannot be truly evangelistic or truly biblical. We cannot be the light of the world unless our ultimate obedience is to Jesus Christ. Too often we have let the values of our society go unquestioned. We hesitate to deal with the troublesome problems of materialism, militarism, and racism. In so doing, we are in danger of equating the American way with the Christian way of life and disobeying the command, "Be not conformed to this world."

We must liberate ourselves and the Church from such conformity to the world and allow ourselves to hear the Word of God penetrating through the confused, groping voices of society.

Chapter 8

Faith
and Violence

THE MOST agonizing decision I have ever had to make in public office came shortly after my election as Governor in 1958. A man was being held in the penitentiary, convicted of a most gruesome murder, guilty beyond credible doubt, and sentenced to die.

I was firmly opposed to capital punishment, and had publicly so stated. However, the state, through the legislature, had considered a proposal to repeal capital punishment. The opinions of the people of Oregon were clearly reflected in a decision against any such repeal; the people favored capital punishment.

As Governor, I possessed the legal power to commute the man's sentence. Yet, I had taken an oath of office which bound me to uphold the state's Constitution and its laws. And in this case, there seemed little doubt about what faith-

fulness to the intent and spirit of laws recently upheld would
dictate.

I spent hours in prayer and in deep personal anguish.
Finally, I decided that the trust which the people had placed
in me to represent their will must be honored, notwithstanding the conflict with my personal convictions. So I did not
exercise the power to commute his sentence, and the execution took place as ordered by the court. As Governor, I believed this fulfilled my constitutional responsibility to carry
out justice on behalf of the people of Oregon.

There are no doubts in my heart that I reached the most
prayerful and responsible decision possible. I felt then a sense
of rightness about it, despite the deep anguish. I have had
the inner assurance that I made the best judgment, following
in genuine earnestness the oath of office I had taken.

Nevertheless, if faced with that decision today, a decade
and a half later, I question whether my choice would be the
same. Now, by acknowledging as a higher duty the prior
dictates of my conscience and my faith rather than my obligations to the majority will of the people, I might rather
render first unto God rather than unto Caesar.

What is the relationship between conscience and law?
What is the meaning of justice, how does that relate to forgiveness and love? Think, for instance, of the angry outcry
at the pardon of Richard Nixon throughout the nation because "justice had not been done." To what extent should
a politician in a representative democracy guide his or her
actions by the popular opinion of the people? When and
why should a public official—and particularly a chief executive—act contrary to the intentions of the people?

Lying beneath these considerations, however, particularly
for the Christian, is the central question of violence.

Like most of my peers, I grew up in a time when the high-
minded and utopian dreams of pacificism for the world were
shattered by Hitler's Blitzkrieg. The world was not getting
better and better every day, and laying down our swords
would not bring the assurance, promised by some, of a world
free from evil and war. Joining the Navy, I fought in the
Pacific against the Japanese, and then, after Japan's sur-

render, was part of the forces attempting to assist Chiang
Kai-shek in the Chinese Civil War; that brought me to
mainland China and also to Vietnam. It was all a duty which
seemed morally necessary. My convictions about the immorality and futility of imperialistic wars, such as the French
attempt to reenter Indochina, were galvanized, and I was
sensitized to the untold suffering of humanity's hungry and
poor masses of people. But war itself? At the time, it was a
necessary, though abhorrent, evil; we felt a patriotic duty to
serve, and even a clear sense of righteous mission.

In the war's immediate aftermath, however, one vivid
experience made the profoundest impression on me. I was
with a Navy contingent who were among the first Americans
to enter Hiroshima after the atomic bomb had been dropped.
Sensing in that utter devastation the full inhumanity and
horror of modern war's violence, I began then to question
whether there could be any virtue in war.

In my childhood exposure to Christianity and in the Baptist church I attended when I came home from the war,
service of the country in the armed forces was a spiritually
blessed duty and privilege. This was never posed to me as
any basic conflict for the Christian. As the cold war emerged,
the moral and spiritual sanction behind our preparation for
war was given a new justification.

Vietnam fundamentally challenged the synthesis between
faith and a nationalistic call to war. Partly because of my
past experience in Indochina, I felt that the moral case
against our involvement was overwhelming. Christian doctrines allowing for "just wars" would clearly prohibit what
we were doing there. As I explored these questions in light
of my Christian faith, even more fundamental considerations
could not be dismissed. I began asking whether and how
the Christian's active participation in violence and war ever
could be justified.

Studying the Bible for its views of the State as well as early
Church history unavoidably brought me up against the issue
of violence. I had affirmed, as shared earlier, that our allegiance as Christians to any State is conditioned by our
commitment to a higher authority, to God. If Christ is truly

Lord, his revelation has given us a normative guide for our own lives, and an authority above all others.

Christ came proclaiming the Good News of God's Kingdom—the promise of a new way of life which comes through obedience to God, and can be known through following Jesus as Lord. This life begins now on earth, in our present milieu; its final and complete fulfillment comes at the end of time, in eternity.

Christ taught clearly the attitudes and commitments which characterize this Kingdom, or this new life; its blueprint is given most clearly in the "Sermon on the Mount." In Matthew's account, Christ gives his disciples the "beatitudes," and tells them they are the true light of the world, encouraging them to be like salt with savor, and like lamps whose light bursts forth in the open (Matt. 5:1–16).

Then Jesus' words seem to reach out to the larger crowd which has gathered; in Luke's record Christ prefaces his ɪemarks following the beatitudes with, "But to you who hear me, I say . . ." (Luke 6:27). In Matthew, it can be inferred that Christ's words were directed to the crowds, most likely directly after the beatitudes; at the end of the whole sermon Matthew writes, "When Jesus had finished this discourse the people were astounded at his teaching . . ." (Matt. 7:28).

Christ described at this point the quality of life and righteousness which was to characterize those called to follow him and be a part of his Kingdom. A core of his teaching dealt with the question of violence:

> "You have learned that they were told, 'Eye for eye, tooth for tooth.' But what I tell you is this: Do not set yourself against the man who wrongs you. If someone slaps you on the right cheek, turn and offer him your left. If a man wants to sue you for your shirt, let him have your coat as well. If a man in authority makes you go one mile, go with him two. Give when you are asked to give; and do not turn your back on a man who wants to borrow.
>
> "You have learned that they were told, 'Love your neighbour, hate your enemy.' But what I tell you is this: Love your enemies and pray for your persecutors; only so can you be children of your heavenly Father, who makes his sun rise on

good and bad alike, and sends the rain on the honest and the dishonest. If you love only those who love you, what reward can you expect? Surely the tax-gatherers do as much as that. And if you greet only your brothers, what is there extraordinary about that? Even the heathen do as much. There must be no limit to your goodness, as your heavenly Father's goodness knows no bounds" (Matthew 5:38–48).

The same attitude of self-giving love is prescribed for other aspects of ethical responsibility.

In his words, Christ first sets forth the predominant religious understanding of the day: "You have learned that they were told. . . ." Then he contrasts these popular notions of cultural morality with the righteousness of the Kingdom he came to inaugurate: "But what I tell you is this. . . ."

The lives of those who follow Christ are to be markedly distinctive in the purity of their love from the Pharisees and the doctors of the law, who were the definers of upright behavior in that society (Matt. 5:20). He calls for a fundamentally new way of embodying God's love and relating to others in society. We are not to avenge or retaliate against wrongdoing: in fact, we are not even to resist the evil another inflicts upon us. Instead, we are asked positively to love our enemies and actively to pray for them.

This is how we are to be the "children of the heavenly Father." His love is total and unconditional: it reaches out to all, and the benefits of his grace are given to good and bad alike (5:45). If we are truly his sons and daughters, then our love will be like his; our love can know no limits because our Father's goodness knows no bounds nor conditions (5:48).

Christ's teaching about the forsaking of revenge and violence and replacing it with love for one's enemies is without qualification. Living under this mandate, how can we maim or injure anyone, and how can we take part in war and kill others?

Someone—I believe Nietzsche—said that all Christian theology consists of attempts to explain away the Sermon on the Mount without destroying faith. How ironic it is that Chris-

tians who fight the hardest to preserve a "literal" interpretation of the Scripture balk at taking literally the most crucial
sermon of their Lord.

We dismiss the concrete relevance of Christ's words by
suggesting that they are not meant to apply to our own time.
Some within the "liberal" theological tradition have done
this by claiming that Jesus' disciples lived with the fervent
expectation that the end of all history was just around the
corner. Christ's teaching is not understood, then, as an attempt to spell out a practical ethic for society in all times.
Rather, the best we have are some idealistic but often impractical principles to bear in mind while establishing our
ethical stance in contemporary society.

This seems to denigrate not only Christ's divinity, but also
his humanity. Did not Christ come in the flesh, entering
into the concrete world of history, politics, culture, and full
humanity, in order to demonstrate how life is intended to
be lived? Was he not "like us in all ways, except without
sin"? If he fully entered into our human predicament and
then told us to love our enemies, how can we decide that
this part of his life is not central to us in our time? Are we
to let the "realities" of our age determine which commands
of Christ should be heeded today, and which should not?
Would not that make us guilty of exactly what Christ condemned—letting the prevailing, relative notions of a society's
ethic, rather than a transcendent vision of God's Kingdom,
be the basic starting point for guiding one's attitudes and
actions? We too easily neglect the full humanity of Christ
and erode his divinity as well by believing that a crux of his
teaching is not directly applicable to those who name him
Lord today.

Some fundamentalists, on the other hand, have suggested
in certain circles that these words apply only to a future
millennial kingdom, when Christ returns and establishes his
rule over all. The admonition to nonviolent love, then, is
not asked of his disciples today. But this view seems flatly
contradicted by the Scripture and Christ's own words. No
one could plausibly argue that Christ's words about anger,
adultery, divorce, prayer, forgiveness, religious hypocrisy,

money, and judgment, all of which are addressed in this discourse, should not be taken with utter seriousness by his followers today. On what grounds, then, are we exempt from obeying the ten verses of this teaching (Matt. 5:38–48) which addresses the love of one's enemies?

At the end of Christ's sermon in Matthew he says:

> "What then of the man who hears these words of mine and acts upon them? He is like a man who had the sense to build his house on rock. The rain came down, the floods rose, the wind blew, and beat upon that house; but it did not fall, because its foundations were on rock. But what of the man who hears these words of mine and does not act upon them? He is like a man who was foolish enough to build his house on sand. The rain came down, the floods rose, the wind blew, and beat upon that house; down it fell with a great crash" (Matt. 7:24–27).

We find the same message at the conclusion of the shorter version of this discourse recorded in Luke 6:20–49. Further, Christ charged his apostles at the ascension to make disciples everywhere, baptize them, and "teach them to observe all that I have commanded you" (Matt. 28:20).

Finally, as was pointed out to me in a most helpful paper I received from Dr. C. Gary Staats, a former teacher at the Multnomah School of the Bible in Portland, Oregon, the problems Jesus addresses in this sermon would not be confronted in any future millennial kingdom:

> All the things discussed in the Sermon are strange indeed to a period when the lamb and the lion will lay down together (Isa. 11) and when universal peace is going to reign as the millennial period according to Old Testament Scripture anticipates. Smiting one in the face, being compelled by government, and Christians being persecuted are not going to be occurring in this future period according to previous Old Testament revelation (Micah 4; Isa. 2:1–4; 11 etc.).

Both liberal and fundamentalist rationalizations for disregarding Christ's clear words about loving one's enemies are shallow evasions of discipleship.

Because of what seems to be the pragmatic impracticality
of nonviolence, I have struggled hard to find some reason for
not fully hearing these words. Yet, I have found no completely comfortable way of pretending Christ did not mean
what he said. Christ's own life gives us the exegesis of his
words; through what he did we can see clearly the meaning
of what he said. His love and obedience to God's will led
him to the cross, where he suffered for the sake of all humanity. He went to the cross rather than fight because his
Kingdom was based on God's boundless love rather than
the sword. There, he breathed in his parting breaths a prayer
of forgiveness for those who put him to death. "Father, forgive them: they do not know what they are doing" (Luke
23:34). He seemed utterly vulnerable and totally crushed.
Yet never has love had such power; never has victory been
so overwhelming.

The "weakness" of his love totally triumphed over the
"strength" of their hate. Christ met and overcame the power
of the world's sin not by killing nor by inflicting evil, but by
taking on the suffering caused by evil and returning it with
love.

In the death and resurrection of Christ, we see that God's
love has the last word. That love was never compromised;
evil was never returned by evil, but with a compassion
grounded in the Father's love.

Part of the defeat of sin was its inability to provoke a
sinful response from God's Son. Though even inflicting
death, its power was overcome by the resurrection. Christ
was made Lord over all, sovereign over all history:

> Let your bearing towards one another arise out of your life
> in Christ Jesus. For the divine nature was his from the first;
> yet he did not think to snatch at equality with God, but made
> himself nothing, assuming the nature of a slave. Bearing the
> human likeness, revealed in human shape, he humbled him-
> self, and in obedience accepted even death—death on a cross.
> Therefore God raised him to the heights and bestowed on
> him the name above all names, that at the name of Jesus every
> knee should bow—in heaven, on earth, and in the depths—

and every tongue confess, 'Jesus Christ is Lord,' to the glory of God the Father (Phil. 2:5–11).

Paul tells us that "the doctrine of the cross is sheer folly to those on their way to ruin, but to us who are on the way to salvation it is the power of God" (1 Cor. 1:18). Here the glory and power of God have been supremely revealed; and here we find the only power to live both now and eternally, as God's redeemed people.

The New Testament tells us continually that we are to live following our Lord, and with his love; we are to respond to evil as he did, and our lives are to take the shape of his.

> Christ suffered on your behalf, and thereby left you an example; it is for you to follow in his steps. He committed no sin, he was convicted of no falsehood; when he was abused he did not retort with abuse, when he suffered he uttered no threats, but committed his cause to the One who judges justly. In his own person he carried our sins to the gibbet, so that we might cease to live for sin and begin to live for righteousness. By his wounds you have been healed. You were straying like sheep, but now you have turned towards the Shepherd and Guardian of your souls (1 Pet. 2:21–25).

Romans 12:17 to 13:10 makes it clear, as we have seen before, that we are to "never pay back evil for evil," as does 1 Thessalonians 5:15.

Ephesians 4:13, 5:12, Philippians 2:5, Romans 15:2–3, and many other texts instruct us to embody our Lord's life and love.

> We for our part have crossed over from death to life; this we know, because we love our brothers. The man who does not love is still in the realm of death, for everyone who hates his brother is a murderer, and no murderer, as you know, has eternal life dwelling within him. It is by this that we know what love is: that Christ laid down his life for us. And we in our turn are bound to lay down our lives for our brothers. . . . My children, love must not be a matter of words or talk; it must be genuine, and show itself in action (1 John 3:14–16; 18).

He loved us while we were still his enemies; so we are to love our enemies. Here we see the profound and revolutionary implications of the atonement: God's love through Christ came to humanity—to each of us—in spite of our sin, and with no conditions; it came even though we did not merit love. We who are justified by this atonement are then to extend this same love to all others in our witness to our faith in Christ's redeeming power.

Believing that Christ's teaching and example, as well as his atoning death and resurrection, set forth unequivocally the way of nonviolence for his followers invariably prompts objections and doubts from fellow Christians. What about the wars in the Old Testament? Did not God command the Israelites to fight? Then, what about Christ in the temple? Or his words to the disciples shortly before his arrest asking whether they had swords? These are the primary objections which are raised from Scripture. Let me share my thinking about them as I have struggled with this issue.

At the beginning of the Old Testament, we have the record of sin's entry into the life of humankind in the Garden of Eden. After eating the forbidden fruit, the first recorded concrete act by those in Genesis which demonstrated humankind's sinful condition was Cain's murder of Abel. His self-righteous protest epitomizes the depth of sin that has entered humanity: "Am I my brother's keeper?" (Gen. 4:9). The belief that we have no responsibility for the welfare of other persons created by God and that we can even kill them is condemned through this incident at the outset of Scripture as sin.

Throughout the Old Testament we find instances of the prophets warning the nation of Israel about its warring intentions. From Hosea, for instance, we read: "Because you have trusted in your chariots, in the number of your warriors, the tumult of war shall arise against your people, and all your fortresses shall be razed . . ." (Hos. 10:13–14). We hear a similar warning from Isaiah: "Shame upon those who go down to Egypt for help, and rely on horses, putting their trust in chariots many in number and in horsemen in their

thousands, but do not look to the Holy One of Israel or seek
guidance from the Lord!" (Isa. 31:1).

In Jeremiah, we read the startling case of how he coun-
seled against an alliance with Egypt opposing Nebuchadnezzar, the king of Babylon, who had conquered the Israelites.
Jeremiah contended that the plight of the Israelites was
the result of God's judgment and was not to be opposed. This
was part of the reason for Jeremiah's imprisonment.

In addition to the prophets' words of warning about war,
the messianic prophecies give us words of promise about the
peace which God intends for his people. The Messiah will
be a "Prince of Peace" (Isa. 9:6); part of Isaiah's vision is
this promise:

> . . . They shall beat their swords into plowshares, and their
> spears into pruning hooks; nation shall not lift up sword
> against nation, neither shall they learn war any more. (Isa.
> 2:4, RSV).

The same promises are recorded in the Psalms:

> O God, endow the king with thy own justice. . . .
> May hills and mountains afford thy people peace. . . .
> May he have pity on the needy and the poor. . . .
> May he redeem them from oppression and violence
>   (Ps. 72:1, 3, 13, 14).

> Come and see what the Lord has done,
> the devastation he has brought upon earth,
> from end to end of the earth he stamps out war:
> he breaks the bow, he snaps the spear
> and burns the shield in the fire (Ps. 46:8–10).

> Let me hear the words of the Lord:
> are they not words of peace,
>   peace to his people and his loyal servants
>   and to all who turn and trust in him? . . .
> Justice shall go in front of him
>   and the path before his feet shall be peace
>   (Ps. 85:8, 13).

These are only representative passages to demonstrate that the Old Testament does not provide us with a picture of a God who delights in war, but rather a God who abhors war and promises his people peace.

It is no wonder, then, that King David is told by the Lord that he cannot build the Lord's temple; David explains this to his son Solomon:

"I had intended to build a house in honour of the name of the Lord my God; but the Lord forbade me and said, 'You have shed much blood in my sight and waged great wars; for this reason you shall not build a house in honour of my name' " (1 Chron. 22:7–8).

Despite these clear words from the Old Testament, it must be acknowledged that the Israelites fought in wars, seemingly with God's blessing. I was thinking about this issue when I came across a helpful paper written in 1971 by David W. Bennett, a student at Fuller Theological Seminary, titled "God, State, and War." He brought out the distinction between what God permitted among the people of Israel and what he desired. Other Christians writing on this topic have also emphasized God's mighty acts of deliverance for the people of Israel which came when the people trusted the Lord's intervention in history, rather than their own military efforts.

In Egypt, it was God who made his own warfare and judgment fall on the Egyptians through the ten plagues. Having secured their freedom from bondage, the Lord led them to the Red Sea. There again, it was his work which first moved the pillar of cloud to protect the Israelites, and allow them to cross the waters. Moses had told them:

"Have no fear; stand firm and see the deliverance that the Lord will bring you this day; for as sure as you see the Egyptians now, you will never see them again. The Lord will fight for you: so hold your peace" (Exod. 14:13–14).

Once in the wilderness, the Israelites struggled to maintain their faith in God's miraculous guidance. Frequently, they

failed, and at times they found themselves at war, but not
war which the Lord directed them to enter.

When the Lord then gave his promise to continue to lead
his people to the Promised Land, he said:

> I send an angel before you to guard you on your way and to
> bring you to the place I have prepared. . . . If you will only
> listen to his voice and do all I tell you, then I will be an enemy
> to your enemies, and I will harass those who harass you. . . .
>
> I will send my terror before you and throw into confusion
> all the peoples whom you find in your path. I will make all
> your enemies turn their backs. I will spread panic before you
> to drive out in front of you the Hivites, the Canaanites and
> the Hittites (Exod. 23:20, 22, 27–8).

The Lord's pattern is to ask his people to trust in him
for their deliverance and safety. He will fight their enemies
through supernatural acts, and will be faithful to his promises. But the Israelites frequently failed to take the Lord's
promise with total seriousness. Instead, they sought to man-
age on their own, and turned to fight their own battles. God
permitted this, but it was not his desire for the people of
Israel.

As the history of the Israelites continued, we see how
God's intervention on their behalf was maintained, even
during times when the Israelites went forth in violent battle.
But because of the unfaithfulness of Israel, the Lord either
allowed them to make war, or brought enemies who made
war upon them. Yet, he was still faithful, and promised to
deliver them, if the people put their trust in his power
and love.

When such trust in him was given, the Lord performed
his mighty acts of deliverance. Gideon's three hundred men
defeated the Midianites without a battle by following God's
instructions (Josh. 6–7). In 2 Chronicles 20, the people of
Israel were led by their prophet in a singing procession to
meet their would-be attackers, only to find that their enemies
had fought and destroyed each other. Elisha's singular faith
and prayer saved him and Israel from the Syrian armies, and
through God's intervention they were sent home with a

feast, no less, and without any bloodshed (2 Kings 6). Another miraculous rescue from the Syrians came when the Lord caused them to hear the sounds of great armies, and they fled in fear (2 Kings 7). Such faithful trust in the Lord is proclaimed by Zechariah: "Neither by force of arms nor by brute strength, but by my spirit! says the Lord of Hosts" (Zech. 4:6).[1]

This view, then, asserts that a lack of trust and faithfulness on the part of the people of Israel, rather than the clear directive of God, brought them into warfare. It provides a most helpful perspective on the Old Testament which has frequently been overlooked by Christians today who search for a biblical justification of violence and war.

Nevertheless, for those who may still not find this explanation totally satisfactory, other perspectives should be added.

War was seen in the Old Testament as a means of judgment on a particular people. At times, the Israelites themselves came under the judgment of God for their unfaithfulness, and other peoples made war against them. In other cases, the people of Israel carried out God's judgment in their wars against others. Thus, the wars which God did permit or allow were wars fought against those who were God's enemies. But that was not synonymous with every enemy of Israel: we have already seen how Jeremiah spoke God's judgment against an alliance and war seen as essential for Israel's self-preservation.[2]

In this same vein, the wars fought in by the people of Israel resulted from the process by which this people were chosen and used uniquely by God in history. We must understand them in the context of God's covenant with his people. Making any analogy to the situation of present nations becomes impossible. God has not chosen any particular modern state in a special covenant relationship to accomplish his purposes in history. He has chosen the Church, the Body of Christ, for that end, and it does the work of God in the world precisely by its degree of faithfulness to Christ, and his way of nonviolent, suffering love.

For Christians to claim that because the people of Israel fought in war, so we can join our nation in making war on others is unbiblical and heretical. That supposes once again our nation is chosen as was Israel; the result is the worst kind of national idolatry. We cannot assume that the enemies of God are coincidentally the enemies of our own nation, or that Americans have been divinely appointed to carry out the judgments of God in the world.

The wars in the Old Testament were never recorded in order to justify the warfare and violence of modern nations. Rather, they are a testimony to the unfaithfulness and sinfulness of humanity, including God's own chosen people. We see God's judgment reflected through war as the Lord of history continued to achieve his purposes, in spite of sin. Then, we learn of God's continuing faithfulness to humanity through his promises "to guide our feet into the way of peace." [3] This he fulfills through the life, death, and resurrection of his own Son.

In Christ's Sermon on the Mount his format was to cite first what had been taught as the Law and then give the greater revelation and fuller meaning. For instance, Christ refers to the ease with which divorce could be obtained according to the Pharisees' interpretation of Old Testament Law. He then gives a far different and more rigorous view of marriage and divorce (Matt. 5:31–32).

Old Testament grounds for divorce do not override Christ's more specific words. Also, the Old Testament portrays servants of God, including Abraham, who had more than one wife. Certainly we do not emulate their example, irrespective of what Christ taught about faithfulness in monogamous marriage. The same is true with the observance of the Sabbath, and numerous other realms of ethical behavior for the Christian.

With regard to violence and war, Christ specifically tells us that any interpretation of the Old Testament, such as that offered by the Pharisees, or other similar ones suggested today, which justifies returning evil with evil or which justifies the hatred of one's enemies, is totally without foundation and contrary to God's love. Christ came to complete the Law and the prophets (Matt. 5:17); from him we see the true intention and fulfillment of God's redemptive work

through history. The final answer to those who suggest that
the Old Testament can justify the Christian's participation
in violence comes from Christ's own words:

> "You have learned that they were told, 'Eye for eye, tooth for
> tooth.' But what I tell you is this: Do not set yourself against
> the man who wrongs you. . . .
> "You have learned that they were told, 'Love your neighbour,
> hate your enemy.' But what I tell you is this: Love your
> enemies" (Matt. 5:38–39; 43–44).

What, then, about Christ's action in the temple (Matt.
21:12–13; John 2:13–18)? Was he not then engaging in
violent action? Nothing in the scriptural texts clearly suggests that Christ's actions were violent against others. The
reason for Christ's indignation, according to some biblical
commentators, was that the religious leaders of the day were
rejecting the animals for sacrifice brought to them by poor
common people, and then selling those animals for a profit.
It was a scheme which made a mockery out of God's concern
for the poor, and was blasphemy in the house of the Lord.

Jesus responded by making a scourge out of ropes, and
driving the sheep and goats, along with their sellers, out
of the temple. It seems apparent that this was done by using
the scourge on the animals, not on the men who sold them.
The text supports this: "Jesus made a whip of cords and
drove them out of the temple, sheep, cattle, and all. He
upset the tables of the money-changers, scattering their coins.
Then he turned on the dealers in pigeons. 'Take them out,'
he said; 'you must not turn my Father's house into a
market'" (John 2:15–16). If he had used his whip against
the dealers of sheep and cattle, then why not against the
dealers in pigeons? He used words of rebuke against them,
and presumably against the others as well; the scourge he
made on the spot would hardly have been very useful against
other than the animals.

It takes a disregard for much of the New Testament, and
a rather dramatic jump from overturning tables to dropping
bombs in order to use this passage as justifying the Chris-

tian's participation in violence and war. There is not the scriptural evidence to argue from this incident to conclude that Jesus acted in disobedience to what he said. Asserting that he did is to claim that he, like the Pharisees, was a hypocrite.

What this incident does demonstrate is that Christ's call to nonviolence is not a disengagement from the injustice in the world; it is not a withdrawal into an irrelevant, pious quietude that shuns any confrontation with evil. Rather, our Lord's call thrusts us into the heart of the world's sin and suffering. The compassion of Christ could not simply co-exist with injustice; it embodied God's justice and righteousness, and unavoidably clashed with the corporate sin of the world. That clash culminated in the victory of the cross and the resurrection.

This encounter from Christ's life, as well as his rebuke to the Pharisees in Matthew 23, demonstrates that Christ's love was not passive but active. It meant concrete action against that which blasphemed God's justice and righteousness. In his life, such action went so far as this dramatic and disruptive means of protesting against public sin. If we truly wish to make an instructive example out of Christ's action in the temple, we will not find support for marching off to war or keeping a gun in our bedroom; rather we will find ourselves judged by the timidity and cowardliness that characterizes our commitment to stand against the world's injustices and sin for the sake of Christ.

The final objection likely to be raised from Scripture by believers who doubt the clarity of Christ's nonviolent teaching and example is from Luke 22:35–38:

> He said to them, "When I sent you out barefoot without purse or pack, were you ever short of anything?" "No," they answered. "It is different now," he said; "whoever has a purse had better take it with him, and his pack too; and if he has no sword, let him sell his cloak to buy one. For Scripture says, 'And he was counted among the outlaws,' and these words, I tell you, must find fulfillment in me; indeed, all that is written of me is being fulfilled." "Look, Lord," they said, "we have two swords here." "Enough, enough!" he replied.

This incident takes place immediately after the Last Supper, and before Jesus and his disciples go to the Mount of Olives to pray; later that night Jesus is betrayed and arrested. Some argue that Jesus' words about swords are a justification for the use of violence, at least in self-defense, against one's enemies. We must remember, however, what actually happened. When the chief priests, soldiers, temple police, and others came to arrest Jesus, his followers said, "Lord, shall we use our swords?" (Luke 22:49) Peter, in fact, did, cutting off the ear of the High Priest's servant. But Jesus said, "Put up your sword. All who take the sword die by the sword" (Matt. 26:52). In Luke, Christ replied, "Let them have their way" (22:51), and then proceeded to heal the servant who had been wounded by the sword.

The one certain conclusion to draw from Jesus' earlier reference to swords is that he was not advocating their use, either for a righteous cause, or in self-defense. That should be obvious anyway, for two swords would hardly be adequate even for self-defense against the arresting contingent of police and soldiers. In all four Gospels the thrust of the narrative dealing with Jesus' arrest is his willingness to be delivered into the hands of sinful men, renouncing and condemning any means of violent resistance. Christ's words make vivid the contrast between his example and the violent spirit of those who arrested him: "Do you take me for a bandit, that you have come out with swords and cudgels to arrest me?" (Matt. 26:55; Mark 14:48; Luke 22:52).

Why, then, do these words appear at all in Luke 23:35–38? What do they mean? There are two possibilities. First, Christ was probably emphasizing that the future for the disciples would be one of persecution and hardship. The world would often reject and even kill them, just as he was about to die. From now on, they would not find the open acceptance previously given them. Thus, they should be prepared for such estrangement from the world; in metaphor, to carry one's own purse, pack, and sword—just what a traveler into a foreign or strange land during those days would do. Likewise when Jesus spoke in Matthew 10:34–39 about having come "not to bring peace, but a sword," and then warned that allegiance to him might conflict with even the bonds of family, the meaning is the same. In both cases, Christ used symbolic language in order to explain the cost of discipleship. In Luke 22, the disciples simply did not grasp the full meaning of what Christ was saying.

These verses may be understood a second way: as reflecting accurately the real temptation within Christ and his disciples to use violence as a means of bringing in God's Kingdom. With Zealots numbered among Christ's disciples, there would be strong sentiment to meet the growing confrontation with the power structure by violent force. As we have said earlier, even Christ may have struggled with this temptation as he prayed in the garden that night. From this perspective, these verses in Luke become perfectly understandable. Christ knew that he was to be "counted among the outlaws" (22:37). His life, committed to those who were oppressed, downtrodden, and outcast, caused him to be identified with such outlaws of society as the Zealots. Realizing the Zealot sympathies among some of his disciples, Christ did not reprimand their possession of swords, but did sharply restrain them, saying that two swords was "enough." The full meaning of his approaching death and resurrection would not be clear to his disciples until later. Now, they were still clinging to messianic hopes that Christ would violently seize political power; a few hours later, when he gave himself up without a struggle, they all deserted him.

Christ gave himself in this nonviolent way, saying, "Let the Scriptures be fulfilled" (Mark 14:50), in order to follow God's will and become, on the cross, the atonement for the sins of the world, and the means for our redemption. The way in which his love confronted evil—not with violence and evil in return, but with the willingness to sacrifice, suffer, and forgive, loving to the utmost—is the way Christ's followers are to live.

We are to be one with Christ's Spirit, mystically united to his Body. "Dwell in me, as I in you. . . . If you heed my commands, you will dwell in my love, as I have heeded my Father's commands and dwell in his love" (John 15:4, 10). Paul tells the Colossians, "The secret is this: Christ in you,

the hope of a glory to come. . . . Live your lives in union
with him. Be rooted in him, be built in him" (Col. 1:27;
2:6–7). Living with his life and his spirit in our inmost being,
how can we do other than respond to hatred and evil with
love?

Of course, we know that we will fail. His perfect love can
never be fully reproduced in our wounded lives. Yet, that
does not alter our commitment; we do not transpose the
reality of our sin into a standard for ethical behavior. Christ
himself is our frame of reference, and the source of our hope;
by dying at even deeper levels to ourselves, we can become
more alive with new life in him.

I do not pretend to have the answers about how the way
of Christ's love is to take concrete shape in all the real or
hypothetical situations I might face in my personal life. What
do you do, for instance, when someone you love is being
injured by evil? As we have seen from Christ's life, nonviolent love does not entail a withdrawn, passive acceptance
of all evil. Rather, we are to overcome evil—but overcome
it with good, with love. We can try to restrain one from doing
evil to another, but by love, and out of love for both; the
means may even be laying down our lives for our friends.
This is our ultimate recourse, rather than resorting to the
same methods of violence and evil which we are told to
overcome with love.

The final objection to a posture of Christian nonviolence
is that it is ineffective, impractical, and evades a responsibility to shape the course of history. This objection is cultural, however, rather than biblical. At the heart of it lies
the assumption that our action is to be guided by what we
deem to be "effective," what we believe will be practical for
everyone, and by what we determine will steer the course
of history in the direction we wish it to proceed. Those are
values deeply rooted in Western culture. But they are not
rooted in Christian faith.

Christ's life was revolutionary precisely because his actions
were not calculated on efficacy. His call was one of faithfulness to God's will, not obedience to human dictates of what
would "work." To follow that counsel would have meant

throwing his lot in with the Zealots and fighting a war of liberation, or else capitulating to some of the objections raised by the Pharisees or Sadducees in order to gain greater "influence" within some segment of the establishment. It would not have meant going to the cross. That is why Paul writes that the cross is a "scandal" and "sheer folly" to the world's wisdom.

> This doctrine of the cross is sheer folly to those on their way to ruin, but to us who are on the way to salvation it is the power of God. . . . God has made the wisdom of this world look foolish. . . . Jews call for miracles, Greeks look for wisdom; but we proclaim Christ—yes, Christ nailed to the cross; and though this is a stumbling-block to Jews and folly to Greeks, yet to those who have heard his call, Jews and Greeks alike, he is the power of God and the wisdom of God.
>
> Divine folly is wiser than the wisdom of man, and divine weakness stronger than man's strength. My brothers, think what sort of people you are, whom God has called. Few of you are men of wisdom, by any human standard; few are powerful or highly born. Yet, to shame the wise, God has chosen what the world counts folly, and to shame what is strong, God has chosen what the world counts weakness. He has chosen things low and contemptible, mere nothings, to overthrow the existing order (1 Cor. 1:18, 21, 22–28).

Faith calls us beyond doing what seems "effective," for faith "makes us certain of realities we do not see" (Heb. 11:1). For the people of God it has always been this way. Abraham went forth out of his land to an unknown future, by faith; he was ready to offer his own son in sacrifice by faith. Moses left the glories and power of Pharaoh's household by faith, and led the Israelites out of bondage by faith. Jericho's walls fell by faith, and the people of Israel were brought to their New Land by faith. The message, as summarized here from Hebrews 11, is that God acts in response to faith. This is what is truly effective. Faithfulness to our Lord is the ultimate test of our actions. One cannot claim that this produces ineffectiveness; Christ's life has changed the course of all history.

Ours, then, is not the responsibility to "make history"; we are not to assume that history's course is ours to chart. Rousseau, Marx, and countless others claim that as humanity's destiny and duty. But Christians put their faith in One who is Lord over all history and sovereign over the universe. We know that history's true purposes are brought closer to their fulfillment not by our allegiance to some ideology, but through our faithfulness to Jesus Christ.

This may not be the way all will choose. But Christ invites all who will to follow, and promises that they will find true Life.

Chapter 9

The Purist
and the Apologist

CAN HUMANITY engage in politics without violence?

Does a commitment to nonviolence offer any hope to a world which respects only power?

When evil, supported by violent power, oppresses so much of humankind, what hope have those who are in bondage if they do not fight fire with fire?

The cross of Jesus may be carried by those who believe his Gospel; but what relevance has it to an unbelieving world?

Christians can seek to follow their Lord; do you expect a nation, however, to do other than to seek its self-preservation?

Questions like these remain on the agenda of the Christian who accepts a personal call to nonviolence, but who understands the agony of a world still ensnarled by evil and sin.

131

Humanity has tried placing a utopian faith in liberal pacifism; this was crushed by World War II. No longer can we say that pacifism by some will lead to peace for all. The Christian who takes sin seriously never should have made such a mistake in the first place. The nonviolence of Christ did not prevent him from being hanged on the cross. Loving our enemies does not insure that they will become our friends.

Is the answer, then, to abdicate to the realities of power politics in the world, allowing its corporate life to be totally governed by the evil we know is present? I think not. To do so we must pretend that Christ's Word holds no truth for the world, and that his life is monumentally irrelevant to our age.

If we are to follow Jesus as Lord, we must synthesize a commitment to his nonviolent love with the world's evil, its addiction to violence, and the struggle of the oppressed for justice. As I endeavor to do so, from within I hear two voices beckoning me to heed their advice. One I call the "Purist"; the other gives me the counsel of the "Apologist."

The Purist says that I must follow the commands of Christ to their ultimate conclusion. There can be no compromise with a world that bows to the dictates of violence and revenge. My task is not to cooperate with the world in its sin, but to live my life on the basis of self-giving love. Together, Christian believers can show the world how a community can be organized on the principle of mutual love rather than on the basis of fear and coercion. Through that witness, we point to the depth of humanity's true problem, namely, sin and the vacuum of genuine love within the hearts of people. In this way, the Purists are salt, light, and hope to all the world. As the Church, they embody in some clearer, though still vastly imperfect way, the material from which God's Kingdom can begin to take some concrete shape and bear witness to the world.

Yet, the Purist realizes that in a fallen world, those not called to Christ's Kingdom will need to be governed by principles including force and violence. The State performs this function. In the eyes of the Purist, that is part of civil government's intended duty. Police, for instance, are needed to maintain order and justice. But the Purist would not personally perform that function, for those duties of the State which rely on violence are not the Christian's task to execute. That does not necessarily exempt the Christian, however, from meaningful involvement in government. Yet a Purist would not be a President and Commander-in-Chief of armed forces which were committed to meeting nuclear attack with a similarly violent response.

The Purist understands that the State will employ violence for its own preservation. When it comes to internal order in society, the Purist could accept the legitimacy of force as necessary, in principle, to maintaining social coherence and preventing the injustices of anarchy. Accepting that principle, however, never means that anything done by the State in the name of law and order is justified; on the contrary, the Purist warns that most every State is likely to use force more to protect the injustices of the status quo than to establish a true reign of justice.

The Purist can never condone any use of force against other nations. Christ's words are true for all, whether they believe in him or not. Our enemies are to be loved and our persecutors blessed, despite the potential suffering that may be inflicted on those who refuse to hate; the truest form of peace will come about only when we return evil with love. Peace cannot be built through terror, through threats of mutual retaliation, and through war. Such peace will always ultimately fail, the Purist argues, for it supposes that evil can beget good. Nations may temporarily be held in check by the power of their adversaries. But there will come a time when one or the other will become fearless enough, whether through calculation or provocation, to seek victory rather than live with an ambiguous and frustrating stalemate.

To establish peace by a balance of terror is like building a house on sand. The more you work for such a peace, the more people believe that nuclear missiles prevent a holocaust, that armies keep us from fighting, and that peace can be achieved through war.

Gandhi told us that "the means are the end in the making." He was a Purist, yet deeply involved in politics; he liberated, in fact, an entire nation from colonial oppression.

"There is no way to peace," A. J. Muste said. "Peace is the way."

What would happen after all, the Purist asks, if one of the nuclear superpowers said to the other, "If you wish to annihilate us, so be it. But we will not annihilate you in turn, for what would be the point?"

When are the interests of a nation, which often mean its economic prosperity, truly more vital than the lives of people? When are we ever justified in repudiating our fundamental conviction about the worth and dignity of all human life? Is not war the greatest evil, for it makes all of humanity's worst and most heinous crimes justifiable?

If you kill your neighbor you can be executed. But if you slaughter hundreds of "enemies" who were born not next door, but in another country, you are a hero. The Purist wonders how we can blindly accept such a contorted ethic and claim that our culture is "civilized."

Would not humanity be brought closer to true peace if people were willing to resist evil with an inner freedom which could never be destroyed, and with a willingness to endure, to suffer, and even to die rather than to kill? Is not the only sane rock on which to build true peace genuine, sacrificial love?

The voice of the Purist usually falls on deaf ears. Then, isolated from the world and absorbed in the task of building God's new community, Purists can even come to despise the world which their Lord came to save. Sensing the intransigence of society's evil, such pessimistic Purists seem content to let the world be damned. They abrogate their mission and witness to the larger society, with all of its suffering and evil. This stance is disconcerting, for how can we love all people if, fundamentally, we have turned our backs on them?

More faithful Purists, however, learn how to nurture their vision, build their community, and open their hearts to a sinful world with the same compassion and long-suffering that flooded Christ's eyes with tears as he looked out over Jerusalem. Their voice resounds deeply within me, and they speak urgently relevant words to those wedded to the realities of power politics.

The pure apostles of nonviolence, whose lives are united with the Prince of Peace, can offer true words of hope to a world besieged by violence and war. At the heart is the vision of our common humanity, underscored by the atonement. Our highest allegiance transcends the boundaries of nationalism; it is given to the whole world, which God loved so much that he sent his only Son. "Christian nonviolence," Thomas Merton wrote, "is not built on a presupposed division, but on the basic unity of man." [1] We hold forth the prior commitment to love all humanity as essential to peace. While statesmen argue that the interests of their nations are overriding, Christians reply that the interests of humanity are ultimate.

The Purist can point to the possibilities of extending the rule of international law, and thus enlarging the ways that humanity's fundamental commonality is reflected in political structures. The ultimate goal is for the society of nations to live under common law that declares international violence and aggression illegal. As Albert Camus said, "We are not so mad as to think that we shall create a world in which murder will not occur. We are fighting for a world in which murder will no longer be legal." [2] Some Purists become pragmatic or compromised enough to suggest an international police force as a means of upholding the rule of such international law.

In addition to suffering love, the Purist can offer certain concrete options for confronting aggressive evil in the world. There are workable strategies for restraining the dangers of ruthless aggression other than having individual nations arm themselves with monstrous power and then define unilaterally how to use it. That is international anarchy. This current approach must be abandoned if we believe that the reality of our common humanity ultimately transcends the divisions of national sovereignty.

Nevertheless, the hope of what might, could, or should be does not dismiss the present reality of what is. International law exists now only in its most rudimentary forms, and the

United Nations has long been paralyzed from evolving into
a powerful and effective structure for securing world peace
by the "Big Powers," both socialist and capitalist. Does the
Purist have any further word to say to these realities, other
than speaking prophetic warnings about the world's present
precarious plight? I believe so.

Our world is so deeply addicted to violence that it has lost
all objectivity about its actual efficacy and value. Having
developed such psychological and economic needs for their
machines of war, nations are no more capable of exercising
detached and wise judgments about the usefulness of violence
as opposed to other nonviolent alternatives than a junky
could render about heroin.

Knowing this, the Purist pleads for people to understand
historically and strategically, as well as morally, what nonviolence can achieve. The most persuasive case I have seen
to this end is Gene Sharp's massive study, *The Politics of
Nonviolent Action*.[3] This landmark work objectively presents the successes and shortcomings of nonviolent political
action throughout history, and points out to the "realist"
how the objectives sought by nations through war can also
be sought through nonviolent means. The case Dr. Sharp
presents, and which he and I have personally discussed, is
not made on the basis of moral and theological truths; rather,
it rests on history, and on a profound understanding of what
constitutes political power. Thus, it has just as much relevance to Henry Kissinger as it does to the person committed
in principle to nonviolence.

The American Revolution provides a revealing illustra-
tion. When John Adams was asked about that revolution,
he wrote:

> But what do we mean by the American Revolution? Do we
> mean the American War? The Revolution was effected before
> the War commenced. The Revolution was in the minds and
> hearts of the people. A change in their religious sentiments,
> or their duties and obligations. . . .
>
> This radical change in the principles, opinions, sentiments
> and affections of the people, was the real American Revolu-
> tion.[4]

His point was precisely correct; the Revolution was not the war, but the undermining of the legitimacy of British authority over the colonies, and the acts of resistance which followed. Most all these acts were nonviolent. Colonists boycotted British products, disobeyed laws, did not pay taxes, and developed an alternative government during the decade and a half before 1775. In fact, British political authority was completely undermined and replaced in the colonies of Massachusetts and Maryland by that time, before a shot was fired. This was the essence of the revolution. Many suggest that if these tactics had been further expanded, the Revolution could have been successfully completed without armed resistance. Portraying the war as identical to the American Revolution, as happens in the bicentennial year, totally misunderstands the true dynamic and power which forged struggling colonies into a nation.

Revolutions have been completed totally without war. Czarist Russia fell in February, 1917—before the Bolsheviks took power later that year—through strikes, the disregard of the Czar's authority by many groups in society, and other nonviolent means which caused the collapse of the government. Similar tactics overthrew dictatorships in El Salvador and Guatemala in 1944. Nationwide nonviolent action successfully defended the German Weimar government in 1920 from a reactionary *coup d'etat*.[5]

> Throughout history, under a variety of political systems, people in every part of the world have waged conflict and wielded undeniable power by using a very different technique of struggle—one which does not kill and destroy. That technique is nonviolent action.[6]

The record of how nonviolence has been utilized, and how it has affected history is cogently summarized in Sharp's work. Included are the nonviolent efforts against Hitler, which severely limited his ability actually to govern those whom his armies overran in nations like Norway and Denmark, as well as the striking example of Gandhi's nonviolent struggle for independence in India.

Conquering a people is not synonymous with ruling them.
I had often thought that nonviolent means could succeed in
colonial India, where Gandhi could appeal to the British
sense of conscience, but could not succeed against ruthless
dictatorships like Hitler's. Yet, the history of nonviolent
action in the widest variety of cultural and political frame-
works belies such a simplistic analysis. Further, even Hitler
acknowledged the need for his occupying armies to win the
cooperation of those conquered in order to govern:

> Ruling the people in the conquered regions is, I might say,
> of course, a psychological problem. One cannot rule by force
> alone. True, force is decisive, but it is equally important to
> have this psychological something which the animal trainer
> also needs to be master of his beast. They must be convinced
> that we are the victors.[7]

Gandhi pointed out clearly that his strategy could be followed and employed regardless of tyranny of one's oppressors:

> At the back of the policy of terrorism is the assumption that
> terrorism if applied in a sufficient measure will produce the
> desired result, namely, bend the adversary to the tyrant's will.
>   But supposing a people make up their mind that they will
> never do the tyrant's will . . .[8]

The extent to which such tactics can achieve their ends
depends not upon the benevolent character of those being
opposed, but upon the depth of commitment held by those
who are nonviolently struggling against them.
    The security of a nation is not identical to its military
power. Any government's power—democratic or dictatorial
—is not a simple function of its force.

> The power of all governments is derived from sources in
> the society—moral authority, material resources, human re-
> sources, skills and knowledge, intangible factors and sanctions.
> Each of these is directly or indirectly dependent upon the
> attitudes, cooperation, obedience, and submission of people.
>   Withdraw that necessary assistance and the power is weak-

ened; maintain the withdrawal despite repression and the opponent's power may be dissolved.[9]

It is true that as a government increases its means of repression, the cost of nonviolent resistance will also escalate. Then, the counsel offered by the Christian becomes increasingly relevant: namely, that there is unique power in the willingness to suffer, that sacrificial love can be redemptive, and that by being willing to lay down our lives for the sake of others, we can discover true life. "There is no greater love than this, that a man should lay down his life for his friends" (John 15:13).

Does the Purist say, then, that nonviolence should be adopted because it promises to succeed? Ultimately, no. A Christian's commitment to nonviolence, in the end, is based on obedience to Christ rather than the effectiveness of this strategy. The cross of our Lord cannot be evaded; it must be borne. By the same token, the Christian does not endorse nonviolent means of action for any and all causes. Clearly, nonviolent tactics can be employed to oppress as well as to liberate. Further, there is the danger that utilizing these techniques without the undergirding commitment to love may just provide people with a more clever means of hating their enemies, while stopping short of killing them. While that is preferable to outright violence, the Christian Purist cannot live comfortably with that compromise. Christ told us that the nursing of anger against another, in addition to committing murder, will bring us to judgment (Matt. 5:21–22). The true goal is not just the replacing of violence with nonviolence, but the overcoming of hatred with love.

Nevertheless, the Purist can offer to a world sick with sin the option of nonviolent action as a realistic and historical alternative to either passively accepting evil or violently fighting against it.

Believers in Christ can embrace nonviolence out of faithfulness to their Lord. They can authentically ask people and nations to adopt strategies of nonviolence in the simultaneous pursuit of their interests and the best interests of all humanity.

Our nation and our world are so totally captivated by a
trust in violence that it is no wonder any other options are
blocked from our corporate consciousness, even when they
occur in history. If the massive mobilization for war, which
drains our brightest minds, our most advanced scientific
knowledge, and hundreds of billions of dollars, were offset
by just a small fraction of a similarly mobilized effort pursuing organized strategies of nonviolence, the results could be
astounding. They could offer humanity the hope of lifting
from its shoulders the crushing weight of its mushrooming
arsenals of destruction.

The Purist tells me that violence only begets violence, in a
never-ending circle. By trusting in violence, we sow the seeds
of our own destruction, as well as that of others. Humanity's
hope lies with those who, possessed with faith and compassion, break that circle by demonstrating that evil is overcome by love.

I know personally this same word; it addresses me through
the life, death, and resurrection of my Savior.

The other voice I hear within I call the "Apologist." His
counsel is more pragmatic. He yearns to set forth an ethic
based on Christian insight that can be responsibly and
prudently embraced by those enmeshed in the power politics
of the world. The Apologist wants to demonstrate the relevance of Christian faith to the mainstream of society's life.
He knows it is impossible for us, individually or corporately,
to be totally free from sin's bondage; to believe we can is the
most dangerous of delusions. We can, however, seek relative
means of diminishing the scope of sin's reign by acting to
further God's justice in the world, relying on his redemptive
grace.

The Apologist can accept a Christian's personal commitment to nonviolence, but he warns me against believing that
stance can or should be extended to nations. Institutions and
states are not capable of self-giving love, and are not meant
to embody it. Their task is to survive, providing a framework for societal life where individuals will have the option
to act with sacrificial love towards others.

Frequently, the Apologist contends that my commitment to Christ's love can be purely applied, to the extent I am able, in my personal relationships to others. But in my wider social and political responsibilities, I cannot be bound by that ethic, for a nation will understandably seek its own self-interest. Recognizing such inevitable corporate sin, my responsibility is to work for whatever greater measure of justice is attainable. The Apologist asserts that seeking to impose a personal commitment to Christ's sacrificial, nonviolent love on a sinful and secular society would be unjust.

Thus, the Apologist could hold any positions of power in society, including those that actively wield the sword. The task in such positions would be to acknowledge and cooperate with the State's self-interests—security, preservation, and order—but to see that those interests are adjusted to the broader requirements of justice. According to the Apologist, I can personally love my enemies, including the Russians and the Chinese; but corporately, I must uphold the balance of power and arms in the absence of any trustworthy alternative. Mutual nuclear deterrence becomes a necessary evil which best preserves our security in a sinful world.

Whenever he is accused of simply abdicating ethical discrimination to the realities of the world, however, the Apologist protests. Rather, he endeavors to transform those realities, at least partially, through the influence of God's justice and grace.

The State's use of violence and war, then, are not ruled out by the Apologist. He contends that there are times and situations when recourse to war is the most morally responsible behavior, and thus should be supported by Christians. However, the Apologist does not accept the State's judgment about when war or violence are necessary; instead, he normally calls them into question by insisting on far more discriminating and demanding standards. Following this counsel, he contends, need not cause me to abandon a prophetic responsibility toward political power. Not only is that role maintained, the prophetic witness is spoken with enough justifiable realism that its warnings may actually be heard and followed by the State.

The Apologist advocates a "Just War" position. He is quick to point out, however, that the true intent of a just-war theory is to prevent and limit recourse to war, not to sanction it whenever the State wishes. His strongest case is presented to me when he conscientiously applies traditional just-war theory to our contemporary situation.

Most Christians hold at least in principle to this position, believing that war is sometimes necessary and right. Yet, frequently they do not apply in a genuine, rigorous manner the standards of a traditional just-war position. It is my conviction that those who do adhere in principle to this position must examine in practice what it requires.

Some historians argue that a few church leaders began raising the question of war's possible justification as early as A.D. 180, more than a century before Constantine. After Constantine's rise to power, however, Augustine set forth the first fully developed just-war position by a Christian theologian (see chapter 6). Since then, other theologians and church leaders have continually attempted to refine just-war theory. Let us examine, then, in light of this tradition, the general principles which must be considered by any Christian who believes that war can be justified.

First, war is always a terrible evil. It is never good nor glorious. Nothing about a just war makes that war good; it is never more than a necessary evil, necessary because the consequences of not fighting would be even more evil than war itself. The Bible constantly condemns war and equates it with humanity's worst sins. Further, outright militarism always falls under God's judgment, and is never an option for the Christian.

A far different attitude pervades society and infects churches. War is frequently glorified. Righteous in cause, war is seen as virtuous in conduct. History's greatest moments are the wars successfully won. Nations like our own, the Soviet Union, and China look in their history to the wars they have successfully waged as vindicating their deepest purposes and ennobling their national character.

In America we do not mourn over past wars; we extol them. Until Vietnam, we tended to view them all as righteous crusades, even when the motives were obviously tarnished with imperialism, as was the case with the Spanish-American War. Of course, there have been the strong voices of dissent. But they have usually been overwhelmed by the quest for national vindication. Remarkably, Lincoln believed that the Civil War was God's judgment on the nation. But no modern President would express such thoughts about even such a moral disaster as the Vietnam War. Their dominant concern was to keep intact our national self-righteousness.

In theaters and on television we see war portrayed heroically. During the Bicentennial we retrace the battles of the Revolutionary War, reenacting them with patriotic fervor. Millions of dollars are spent on toy guns and games of violence for our children, who can grow up believing that war is natural and even fun. In countless ways, war is honored, and we are taught it is other than evil. Against these delusive contentions and deceiving practices, the Purist and Apologist speak with one voice: the glorification of violence must always be denounced.

Just-war theory maintains that war must always be the last resort, and come only if all other alternatives, including negotiations and compromise, have failed. The Apologist can fully embrace the Purist's recommendations for extending the authority of international law, strengthening the U.N.'s peace-keeping powers, and utilizing strategies of nonviolent action. All these alternatives must be fully explored, and every peaceful solution to a conflict, including compromise and concession, must be attempted before war can be just.

The Purist and the Apologist differ in their counsel only when all the alternatives to violence have been fully exhausted. Even then, the Apologist maintains that war is not justifiable unless it is fought for the right reason. Pure defense of peace with justice is the only legitimate reason in traditional Christian ethics for a just war. In short, war must be motivated by and tempered with a genuine caring for all humanity.

The reasons nations usually and realistically prepare for war are rejected, for they fail to meet this standard. No aggressive war is possible; only war that is truly defensive is allowable. War cannot be fought for the sake of one's economic interests. Neither can it be waged to secure or extend a nation's international political advantage. Wars cannot be fought over reasons of ideology, nor can they be launched as means of vengeance or retaliation. All these motivations are rejected; they do not meet the test of seeking solely the restoration of peace for the benefit of all parties, and for the sake of humanity.

When war is fought, furthermore, it must be marked by an ongoing concern for the enemy. The peace sought by war must be just for the aggressor or the enemy as well. Had that dictum been followed in the aftermath of World War I, World War II might never have been fought.

Finally, a war is not just, according to this position, unless the means utilized for fighting it are consistent with the limited end that is sought—the restoration of a peace with justice for all concerned. Christians who uphold a just-war position have made this point ever since the Bishop of Ambrose excommunicated the Emperor Theodosius, who claimed to be a Christian, for commanding the sacking of Thessalonica, with the killing of many innocent people, before A.D. 400.[10]

What are the concrete implications of a just-war position for Christians in America? First we must recognize that few if any of the wars we have fought meet all the requirements of a just war. Some, such as our intervention in Indochina, fail totally. Others, including World War II, were fought for better ends, yet with disproportionate means such as obliteration bombing in Europe and the use of the atomic bomb in Japan. An American soldier who fought, as did I, against Japan, elaborates further:

What kind of war do civilians suppose we fought, anyway? We shot prisoners in cold blood, wiped out hospitals, strafed lifeboats, killed or mistreated enemy civilians, finished off the enemy wounded, tossed the dying into a hole with the dead, and in the Pacific boiled the flesh off enemy skulls to make table ornaments for sweethearts, or carved their bones into

letter openers. We topped off our saturation bombing and
burning of enemy civilians by dropping atomic bombs on two
nearly defenseless cities, thereby setting an all time record for
instantaneous mass slaughter. As victors we are privileged to
try our defeated opponents for their crimes against humanity;
but we should be realistic enough to appreciate that if we
were on trial for breaking international laws, we should be
found quilty on a dozen counts. We fought a dishonorable
war, because morality had a low priority in battle. The tougher
the fighting the less room for decency; and in the Pacific con-
tests we saw mankind reach the blackest depths of bestiality.

Not every American soldier, or even one percent of our
troops, deliberately committed unwarranted atrocities, and the
same might be said for the Germans and Japanese. The
exigencies of war necessitated many so-called crimes, and the
bulk of the rest could be blamed on the mental distortion
which war produced. But we publicized every inhuman act
of our opponents and censored any recognition of our own
moral frailty in moments of desperation.[11]

Our current military posture throughout the globe is
called into serious question by a just-war critique. The
premises of our "defense" policy rely on being prepared to
go to war in protection of our interests in Western Europe
and in the Pacific, including our bonds with Japan and other
Asian allies. That strategy rests far more on the necessity
to protect our own economic and political ties than on
preserving a just peace for all concerned. The current reasons
for keeping our military power in these areas center on
insuring a political climate advantageous to us, especially
economically, rather than achieving the goals sought by a
just war. We ignored Americans like Herbert Hoover who
warned about the dangers of building a post-war military
policy based on the protection of economic and political
interests throughout the globe rather than the prudently
circumscribed necessities of our own defense.

Our strategic nuclear policy, which fails to renounce the
possibility of our being the first to initiate the use of nuclear
weapons in a conflict, is built on the assumption that nuclear
war is a realistic option. This position is fundamentally chal-

lenged by a consistent theory of just war. As Dr. Arthur
Holmes, Chairman of the Department of Philosophy at
Wheaton College, has written:

> The notion of unlimited war has long been repudiated in
> Christian ethics. . . . Since Hiroshima, Protestant and Catholic
> writers and church bodies of all sorts have spoken out about
> the unlimited and disproportionate nature of nuclear war. It
> might well be morally preferable to suffer defeat than to
> slaughter innocent millions.[12]

Incidents like the recovery of the *Mayaguez,* motivated
obviously by a spirit of retaliation and face-saving, fail utterly to meet what just-war theory stipulates as necessary to
sanction any military action. The same is true about the bulk
of our military aid and assistance flowing to regimes throughout the world.

The Apologist says that the only violence Christians can
support by a State is that employed in a just war, as has been
defined. His aim is to prevent the State from embarking on
any other uses of military power; condoning violence and
war in those other circumstances goes contrary to the clear
tradition of Christian teaching and ethics through the ages.

The Christian who accepts a just-war position has not
found a convenient means for justifying war, nor a rationalization for adhering to the major postulates of U.S. defense
policy and the billions of dollars in arms that are required.
(The same can be said about the defense policies of most
other nations.) When faithfully applied, the just-war stance
calls into judgment the assumptions which commonly under-
gird the entire "defense establishment." In the words, again,
of as firm an evangelical Christian as Wheaton's Dr. Holmes,
this position,

> . . . calls for a spirit of Christian internationalism to replace
> the easy equation of conservative religion with the conserva-
> tive politics of an overly nationalistic Americanism. "The na-
> tional interest" can too easily deteriorate from a needed and
> legitimate concern for the common good to a mask for un-
> adulterated selfishness at whatever costs to others.[13]

Today, those cases where the just-war position can be faithfully applied will more likely sanction the violence of the world's poor and oppressed in their struggle for human liberation than the military actions of the world's most powerful nations. When a political regime of a poor nation is dictatorial, ruthlessly oppressive, allied with economic and political forces that preserve the status quo, and offers no hope to the poor masses, then is not revolution committed to building justice for all a viable alternative? Are not these cases in which the requirements of a just war are fulfilled? Certainly it seems so.

We must not ignore, after all, the ongoing structural violence of a world in which the rich few control a monopoly of the world's wealth, leaving the impoverished masses to suffer. That is violence; the deaths it causes are not from bullets and bombs, but from empty stomachs and hopeless hearts. To oppose such violence is a moral imperative; moreover, this is central to faithful Christian obedience.

If the possibility of a just war is acknowledged, I believe the case for embracing it in actuality should be most persuasively made here. When a fellow Christian from a poor nation tells me that violent revolution is the only option for freeing that country's masses from the incalculable daily toll of human suffering, then I find the just-war stance set forth in its most compelling manner.

Theology which makes this case—"liberation theology"—is in vogue today in many circles, and it is embodied by Latin American priests who become committed and armed revolutionaries, or by black Rhodesian Christians who are ready to fight a guerrilla war for their independence from an oppressive, minority regime. Some conservative theologians are quick to condemn such liberation theology for making the gospel too political and for suggesting that God's Kingdom can be advanced by the sword. But what such criticisms frequently ignore is that liberation theology begins with the just-war theory about when violence is justified, and applies it to sanction the violence of the oppressed. Puritan preachers in America did much the same in justifying the violence of our own revolution two hundred years ago.

To use a just-war position in trying to sanction the armed might of the rich and powerful, but then to turn and condemn the violence of the hungry and the oppressed is hypocritical and self-righteous. If we think that violence can be justified for us, then surely we cannot say it is wrong for them.

Here, it seems to me, is the crucial weakness in the just-war position. Violence and war are the outgrowth of fears and hatreds. We fear those who threaten our economic security; nations are vengeful toward those who humiliate them; revolutionaries hate those who oppress them. The result is an impulse to violence. Once these violent motives take root, we search for a means of justifying them. The urge to believe we can be vindicated in our animosities is overwhelming, for that is how we can project the evil and sin within ourselves wholly onto our enemies, insuring our own self-righteousness. The most tempting way of sanctioning our violent impulses is to cling to a just-war theory. Although its principle is that violence is condoned only when motivated by love, in practice this theory becomes the rationalization for our hate.

Once admitting the potential of a just war, the danger is that the Christian's witness to the State becomes focused on when war is proper, rather than whether it is. The State can always convince itself that a given war meets the requirements of a just war, even if the Christian remains sceptical. In that case they disagree over circumstances, not over principle; then it seems that only our judgments differ, and not our convictions.

Living in a sinful world means recognizing that humanity will attempt to cloak its evil inclinations with the best of reasons. The Christian's task in such a situation is not so much to argue about those reasons, but rather to recognize the underlying sin. Then, through love, we can open the way for repentance, and with it, hope and renewal.

The final questions I have are whether love ever can motivate violence, whether we can turn to war as a means for building true peace, and whether the ends ever do justify the means. A Christian who adheres to the just-war position must be able to reconcile affirmative answers to those questions with faith in Christ as Lord. I question whether that can be done.

The voice of the Apologist does speak with persuasive power and strength. There are situations where I can agree with the perspectives it sets forth. In my struggle to interpret the relevance of Christian faith to the dilemmas of secular politics, the Apologist can offer thoughtful, well-reasoned insights for guiding my thought and action.

There are two general reservations which I feel about the Apologist's advice, however. The first is the rigid dichotomy between personal ethics and political ethics. This leaves me uncomfortable. How can I heed Christ's words when relating individually to others, but ignore them when dealing with social and political problems, including corporate sin in society? It is as if I am asked to adopt one set of convictions when I walk into my church, and another when I walk into the chamber of the U.S. Senate. All this can lead to a troubling theological schizophrenia which seems contradictory to the wholeness of the gospel's truth.

Second, while the Apologist strives to take principles derived from Scripture seriously, he seems far too ready to dismiss the content of central biblical passages, and assert that Christ's life has only a general relevance to ours, rather than a concretely personal one. Here, my personal faith makes me resist so loose a view of Scripture, and reminds me that a commitment to Christ as Lord means that we are to be "born again" in order to embody his love and follow him.

The voice of the Purist also raises some reservations within me. The first is that it can prompt the wrong kind of withdrawal from the world—one that forgets "God so loved the world that he gave his only begotten Son" (John 3:16). Our call is to respond by giving ourselves for the healing of the world, rather than to escape from it. The temptations of a Pharisaical self-righteousness must be firmly resisted with the true humility which characterized Christ. Second, the Purist can advocate solutions which seem impossible for people to accept. That in no way means those solutions are wrong; but there must be a sincere effort to interpret Christian faith to the world in a way that demonstrates it is, indeed, Good News, offering true hope and salvation.

Nevertheless, the Purist speaks to me with a whole and biblically rooted Word.

The Purist and the Apologist are not, in practice, always two irreconcilable extremes. They will speak with one voice on some occasions. The counsel each offers has been heard and followed by Christians through the ages, and still today. My own task is to discern, in the concrete circumstances of my life, where I believe that the "Spirit of Truth" is discovered. We each, in our own ways, face this task. We ask not for the assurance to know beyond doubt what is right, but for the faith to believe we are upheld, forgiven, and sustained by loving grace.

Often I have pondered what kind of a world my four children will find when they reach adulthood in the next decade. The quality of life for all humankind then will depend on how we respond now to these foreboding realities:

— *the rampant pace of escalating nuclear power, accompanied with a blind trust in technological expansion;*
— *the inexorable centralization of political and economic power, especially in the industrialized countries;*
— *the deterioration of our environmental milieu, with the ecological and psychological dangers which result;*
— *the monopoly of the world's food and wealth by a few, with hunger and impoverishment for masses, in light of real limitations to the world's resources.*

The next four chapters explore these issues in a preliminary way.

Each of these four threats reveals at its depth the spiritual void within modern humanity. Meeting these basic challenges requires dramatic changes in actions by governments, to be sure. More fundamentally, however, change which offers authentic hope for our future necessitates a transformation of our consciousness, the embracing of new values for our lives, and a sacrificial commitment to the hurt of all humanity as if it were our own. Nothing short of a spiritual revolution nurtured by faith is required as humanity's deepest need if we are to build hope for our children's future.

Chapter 10

"To See the Earth As It Truly Is"

O<small>N</small> A SEPTEMBER day in 1945 we set out from Kure in a procession of small landing craft for the short trip up the estuary to Hiroshima. We were going there as observers, almost the first outsiders to view the destruction that had been wrought. The trip would take about a day, so all the men had provisions for lunch.

Crowds of curious and frightened Japanese gathered along the shore as we went by; among their number were defeated soldiers still wearing remnants of their uniforms, and wondering about their fate. In the city itself, many of those dead from the bomb and its effects had not been buried.

The men with me had been through Iwo Jima and Okinawa. Though the war had finally ended, little more than a month had passed, and hatred of the enemy still was fierce. Once ashore in Hiroshima, some of the U.S. servicemen

from my ship pulled teeth with gold fillings out of mouths
of dead Japanese for souvenirs and pierced earrings. These
men would return to America to become lawyers, teachers,
ministers and businessmen—patriotic citizens and respected
leaders in their communities.

The devastation I saw in Hiroshima seemed beyond the
comprehension of my mind and spirit; I felt jarred in the
depths of my soul. I was witnessing the effects of a horror
too terrible to imagine. Never would I be the same again;
the shock to my conscience registered permanently within
me.

The force generated by the bomb was measured at from
between 5.3 and 8.0 tons per square yard. It was powerful
enough to shift marble gravestones in the cemeteries, and to
lift and move the concrete roadway on a downtown bridge.
At 380 yards from the center of the explosion, it was later
found that mica, with a melting point of 900 degrees Centigrade, had fused in granite gravestones. At 600 yards from
ground zero gray clay construction tiles, with a melting point
of 1,300 degrees Centigrade, dissolved. At the center, heat
generated by the blast was determined to have been 6,000
degrees Centigrade. It was estimated that 78,150 people died;
13,983 were listed as missing.[1]

Then as now, the atomic bomb symbolized the fundamental modern paradox. As the power of the atom was
unleashed, modern humanity was suddenly struck dumb with
the staggering capability of its scientific and technical resources. Had we, in unleashing the power of nature, found
a weapon that could end the prospects of war through the
sheer might of its destructive capability? For many, there
was such hope. The bomb seemed for them to herald the
beginning of a new technological age—an age in which
science, wedded to technology and industrialism, could insure the world's dreams of boundless wealth, the end of
hunger and suffering, and the beginning of a final sense of
true peace.

Now, thirty years later, hope has dimmed. Under the
shadow of nuclear war the world lives on, fearful and anx-

ious. In the short span of three decades humanity has created a nuclear arsenal beyond our comprehension.

In the United States we have now developed the technological capability of releasing the equivalent explosive power of 655,000 Hiroshima bombs. In a world of nearly four billion people, we have the capacity to destroy over four hundred billion. The United States can, in a matter of moments, deliver a single, thermonuclear explosion with more destructive power than both sides dropped against each other during the four and a half years of World War II.

To the modern age belongs the greatest potential yet known for either salvation or destruction. Nurtured by science and technology, a world has been created in which civilization advances, but only as it hangs in a precarious "balance of terror." In the words of philosopher-historian William Thompson, "We are at one of those moments when the whole meaning of nature, self, and civilization is overturning in a revisioning of history." [2] The crossroads of history have been reached.

Whereas once life moved at a leisurely pace, the culture of the twentieth century now demands that we live in constant motion. Modern life, spurred by science and industrialism, now challenges us to accelerate our pace so that we might adjust to the tempo of discovery. Our culture exhorts us to achieve, and then overachieve.

For proof, we need only note that scientists have discovered more in the last thirty years than in all previous human history; that over 80 percent of all scientists the world has ever known are alive today; that each year over one million scientific papers are published. Daily, we absorb the miracles of modern discovery—pictures from the far reaches of our solar system, footprints in the dust of the moon, the creation of life in an antiseptic test tube. We can only marvel at the speed of scientific and technological achievement.

But our supertechnological era is not without cost. It compels that we must react—physically and emotionally—to survive; to run with life or be swept aside. It demands that we change rapidly, adapting radically and constantly to a pace that constantly accelerates. One need only look at the millions who frantically move through the streets of our large cities, their watches accurate to 1/1000th of a second, to understand the complex rituals of modern life summed up in the simple phrase "rush hour." Psychologically, it is an extraordinary age.

The situation is ironic. Never have we known such wealth, but never have we worshiped wealth more. Never have people been so well educated, but never has the application of their knowledge so threatened humanity's freedom, or clouded their rationality. Never have people possessed the potential to free the world from the ageless threats of hunger and war, but never was the world so hungry, or the threat of war more monstrous.

Industrialism, science, and technology have infected our spirit. They have changed the face of culture and of religion. They have brought us a new way of life. In the nineteenth century, as industrialism expanded throughout Europe, the German philosopher Nietzsche noted both the emotional and physical effects it seemed to be having on society:

> When he [the philosopher] thinks of the general bustle, the increasing tempo of life and the lack of all leisurely contemplation, it almost seems to him as though he detected the signs of a complete uprooting of culture. The waters of religion are receding, leaving behind swamps and stagnant pools; nations are again dividing into opposite camps, with the aim of destroying one another. The sciences, pursued without measure and in blind laissez-faire spirit, are disrupting and dissolving all firm beliefs; states and the educated classes, are carried along by a contemptible economic system. Never was the world more worldly, and never was it poorer in love and goodness.[3]

What has become of civilization since Nietzsche made that prophetic observation some one hundred years ago? Industrialism and technology have expanded at a blinding rate of speed; constant, increasingly destructive wars have plagued us for nearly a century; true religion, stressing the simple joys of peace and compassion, has been theologically assaulted by an idolatrous worship of wealth and power.

In a collective sense, we are threatening to become the emotional by-products of society's one-dimensional exaltation of scientific and technological achievement. Dazzled by material success, we have developed a new religion: the worship of progress itself. Whereas people once looked toward God for salvation, they now direct their daily lives toward the domination of nature and fellow human beings in a ceaseless quest for economic prosperity. The worship of the supernatural, the mystical and unknown element of life, has been transformed into a worship of the visible, the tangible, the synthetic.

Once the rise of technology meant an improvement in humanity's life. Now human lives are dedicated en masse to the advancement and improvement of the technological machinery of progress. Left unhindered in its development and unquestioned in its purpose, technology has flourished, while the importance of the person has declined proportionately. People have become cogs in the machine, investments in the future, commodities to be bought and sold in the burgeoning marketplace; they are the functionaries of progress, and the servants of technology. Abundance and the constant drive for success are blessed, while gentleness, compassion, and contemplation have been forgotten. Even to the casual observer it becomes clear that the new religion of progress has wrought a disturbing mixture of blessings.

An American citizen today can stand on the eastern edge of the continent and look out toward the megalopolis which expands to all horizons. These massive industrial cities, the residences of the modern age, are rimmed by cathedrals of glass and concrete—the symbols of our unquestioned material success. Beneath these buildings that are vacated by nightfall, hidden in the shadows of technological splendor, millions have crowded together. To some, most notably the rich, it is a good life. To the others, crowding brings tension, threats of violence and crime, and the rise of an outward social complexity that defies human terms.

Linking city to city lie the arteries of culture—superhighways built on the dust of towns that held our history and linked us to the past. The highways wind by rivers riddled with poisons, by lakes rendered lifeless by industrial sewage, by mountains that cannot be seen through the yellow haze of the sky or the blinking of neon signs. And still, driven by progress, we develop and exploit; still the modern cathedrals rise, the highways widen, and the land is consumed. "Here were decent godless people," T. S. Eliot once wrote, "their only monument the asphalt road and a thousand lost golf balls." [4] For those who founded their faith on progress, for those who honestly hoped that science would solve all problems and herald the beginning of a more joyful human era, reality now denies their faith.

Three major pressures add to humanity's confusion and grow stronger as science and technology advance.

The initial trauma of the modern age can be summed up in ontological questions. How have I come to be? What is the purpose of my existence? With the theories of Copernicus, Darwin, Freud, and others, one of the greatest theological and philosophical ironies became apparent: through science, humanity was discovering more, and, in our own eyes, was somehow becoming less.

The basis of modern secular faith appears to lie only in the advancement of science and technology. As modern humanity views the deterioration of its environment and the swelling of the nuclear arsenal, that faith falters and gives way to the confusions and anger of one losing hope. "For the secret of life," wrote Dostoyevsky, "is not only to live but to have something to live for. Without a stable conception of the object of life, man would not consent to go on living, and would rather destroy himself than remain on earth, though he had bread in abundance." [5] If there is no answer to the fundamental question of human purpose, humanity is left alone in the cold and silent void of the universe.

The second overriding fear of modern humanity is the developing threats of world-wide ecological crises, along with the social, political, and economic disruption that will inevitably follow such an environmental breakdown. This threat is characterized by the dwindling wealth of global resources, and by the rise of national and international economies built on the blind and reckless need for constant expansion. This threat is inevitable on a planet of finite size where nations encourage and sustain our limitless desire to build, develop and exploit what minerals and land there are left.

Propelling this rush toward material acquisition is a force that has been developing since the advent of the industrial revolution: the belief that universal peace is dependent on expanding world-wide prosperity. The economist E. F. Schumacher has recently addressed, and attacked, this notion:

> The dominant modern belief is that the soundest foundation of peace would be universal prosperity. . . . This . . . has an almost irresistible attraction as it suggests that the faster you get one desirable thing the more securely do you attain another. It is doubly attractive because it completely by-passes the whole question of ethics: there is no need for renunciation or sacrifice; on the contrary! We have science and technology to help us along the road to peace and plenty, all that is needed is that we should not behave stupidly, irrationally, cutting our own flesh.[6]

But the belief that peace can be achieved through universal prosperity rests on an eroding foundation—the world's supply of natural resources—and industrial progress is itself devouring that foundation constantly.

Recently, a team of scientists took all major environmental forces at work in the world today, including population growth, industrial expansion, and natural resource depletion, and tried to determine how long the world might survive this present acceleration of all its systems. In their published report entitled *Limits to Growth,* the Club of Rome stated that if we continue in our present course, environmental systems may plummet toward collapse after the turn of the twenty-first century. Other noted scientists have questioned the findings of the Club of Rome, but few question the fact that we cannot continue to strip the world of its resources at our present rate without inviting eventual repercussions of the most fundamental and catastrophic nature.

How long do we have before catastrophe hits? In the late 1960s, U Thant, Secretary-General of the United Nations, said that his experience led him to believe that only ten years remained in which to develop global policies directed toward averting disaster. In 1970, psychologist and ecologist John Calhoun echoed U Thant's concern. He calculated that only ten to fifteen years remained in which to determine and implement the policies necessary to insure human survival. To relieve this threat humanity will be compelled to alter the centuries-old trend of limitless growth and blind industrial progress.

The final and most intense pressure on modern humanity was evidenced in the desolation I encountered at Hiroshima. That we may—through miscalculation or mistrust—lay waste to history itself through nuclear annihilation is a paramount horror of modern existence. The possibility is not often discussed because its implications are, I think, simply too terrible to consider, and too frightening to comprehend. But the threat remains. Locked in the depth of the continent, insulated from attack, made more and more effective by the application of scientific genius, there wait the emotionless instruments of insurmountable destruction.

The technicians of science in this nation, as well as in others, now chart the "acceptable limits" of nuclear execution. They speak of hundreds of millions being lost in a day; they project "games" of limited, strategic, and total nuclear war; they run these projections through computers, and the machines respond with statistical accounts of world-wide death, or genetic mutation, of survivors huddling below a nuclear wasteland in fallout shelters, or rushing toward escape where there can be none.

The fact that we now live and deal with such horror, that we continue to place our faith in the retaliatory security of a "balance of terror," that we have increased our global destructive capability to the point that it can have no purpose but, in Churchill's words, "to make the rubble bounce," demonstrates the moral bankruptcy of modern civilization. Such knowledge should lay to rest the notion that civilized humanity has been moving toward some higher humanitarian state.

One can hope that war will never come, that future generations will be born and successfully replaced by still others, all living on the edge of nuclear war. But a people cannot exist in the balance of terror forever without expecting terror, irrationality, and fear to become a tragic ordeal and a constant symptom of their life. And should the mathematics of the balance falter, and through some tragic breakdown of men or machine, the missiles be sent, there would be few left to question our motives or to examine our failure.

The lessons of Hiroshima must be borne in mind. Many survivors of the 1945 bomb, with bodies burned nearly to the bone, surrounded by the dead, elected simply to sit in their own waste and grieve. Later, rescue workers from neighboring towns came in to help those who had survived. They brought them to hospitals, healed their wounds, and quieted their fears. Contemporary nuclear war, however, would leave few if any unblemished outsiders. The desolation would cover the earth. Technology has, then, brought us to a point in history where we can wreak such havoc that humanity may abandon its willingness to live.

Despite the clear and present danger that these modern pressures pose, science, technology and industrial development continue to form the pattern of our lives. Notwithstanding the fearful objections of the scientists who created the original atomic bomb, we have proceeded in a rational manner toward the totally irrational end of nuclear proliferation. Again, this technological advancement symbolizes the common belief of progress: if the atomic bomb can be perfected, it shall; if economic growth can continue, it must; if technology can more efficiently control the lives of humanity, it will.

To challenge progress, science, or the purpose of our power is to commit a sacrilege. We continue in haste toward some unknown, reminiscent of Melville's captain, consumed in his frantic drive to find the great whale: "All my means and methods are sane," Captain Ahab says; "my purpose is mad." This is how we are attempting to chart our course through the twentieth century.

In recent times, however, we have seen cultural fragments of a disillusionment with traditional technological values. The most obvious example was the appearance of a "counterculture" in the mid-1960s. Since then, we have witnessed the rise of cultural revolution throughout this country in religion, with the Jesus Movement, in the growth of small intentional communities of people, and in a return to a more simple, natural relationship to nature and the world.

These are psychological reactions. Some would argue that they are meaningless, and the work of malcontents or even revolutionaries bent on destroying or challenging the culture. I do not. Frightened by the rise of a value system alien to the religion of progress, many respond to these new subcultures with confusion, fear, and anger. Some cannot understand the zeal for life, or the simple love of humanity, creation, and God evidenced among those searching for alternative ways of structuring their lives.

The rise of these subcultures was predictable, for they represent human, defensive reactions to an era which has brought humanity close to its limit of endurance. These are the people who did not, or could not, choose to cope with an era in which events and time hurtle by with little opportunity to absorb their significance, or contemplate what they mean. For them, modern life is too big, too impersonal, and it changes too quickly for an individual to believe he or she has an opportunity to control or understand its direction.

Confronted by this feeling, some members of the younger generation have turned inward toward the development of personal relationships that deny the impersonalism of modern life. They turn toward the rediscovery of simpler times, the beauty of nature, and religions that help answer the ontological questions that mass culture has ceased asking.

Tragic evidence exists, however, that many who cannot cope with the modern bustle, who cannot find an inner peace on which to build a calm and fulfilling life, turn toward the escape of drugs, or are tragically disturbed. In 1955 over 1,600,000 Americans were admitted to psychiatric institutions. By 1971 the figure rose beyond four million—nearly a 300 percent increase. The number of boys, ages ten to fifteen, that have been admitted to mental hospitals has increased six times since 1950, compared to a twofold increase in population. There has been a 67 percent increase in the suicide rate in young Americans between the ages of fifteen and twenty-four.

If suffering in the nineteenth century was founded on physical cruelty, slavery, and exploitation, suffering in the twentieth century is compounded by the rise of psychological anxiety and self-alienation. The dangers to freedom in the past were that humankind was locked in the chains that Rousseau had said "shackled men everywhere." The danger of the present is that these chains do not encircle our ankles, but our hearts and minds. In the race toward material wealth we as a society are threatening to make slaves of ourselves once again—slaves to a technological empire of our own making, that threatens both our physical and psychological existence. There is no choice; we must endeavor to change, in the most fundamental way, our present course.

How, then, do we proceed? What is necessary to confront the pressures and fears of modern life? I believe it is a fundamental spiritual reawakening. In an individual and collective sense, we must move toward the spiritual transformation of society.

I am not speaking necessarily of a massive return to institutional religions, but rather a return to an inner personal discovery that reality is spiritual, and rooted in a God who is Love. From this one basic presupposition we learn of our common bond with all humanity; from this one act of faith flow forth openness, compassion, and hope.

Spiritual values must again take precedence over material values; we must again view ourselves as the caretakers of the world, rather than the conquerors of it. Only after such a basic cultural transformation will we be able truly to believe that charity can overwhelm greed, that love can replace hate and indifference, and that swords can be turned into plow-shares. In the hope for such a reawakening, Lewis Mumford, a social historian, has written words which echo my own thoughts:

> For its effective salvation mankind will need to undergo some-thing like a spontaneous religious conversion: one that will replace the mechanical world picture with an organic world picture, and give the human personality, as the highest known manifestation of life, the precedence it now gives to its ma-chines and computers. This order of change from the classic power complex of Imperial Rome to that of Christianity, or, later, from supernatural medieval Christianity to the machine-modeled ideology of the seventeenth century. But such changes have repeatedly occurred all through history; and under cata-strophic pressure they may occur again. Of only one thing we may be confident. If mankind is to escape its programmed self-extinction the God who saves us will not descend from the machine: he will rise up again in the human soul.[7]

Developing technology must be seen as a servant to hu-manity, rather than its master, or its executioner. We can no longer continue in our deification of the state, of our ma-chinery and our power—for the corresponding mass worship of success will inexorably void the true spiritual qualities in humanity.

This redirection will require that we abolish—not dimin-ish—the threats of thermonuclear war and world ecological crises that deepen our mistrust and paralyze the advent of creative change. It will mean that we share a common vision, a vision even sensed, ironically, by the explorers on the moon at the pinnacle of modern technological achievement. From their spectacular vantage point in space, the men of Apollo 8 looked toward earth, and saw a strange pearl of life resting quietly in the infinite blackness of space. Archibald MacLeish put the vision in words:

> To see the earth as it truly is, small and blue and beautiful, in that eternal silence where it floats, is to see ourselves as

riders on the earth together, brothers on that loveliness in the eternal cold, brothers that know now they are truly brothers.[8]

From such a simple, mystical vision comes a message that transcends all war, all irrationality, and all petty human conflict. If we can see nothing else, we must begin to understand how precious, wonderful, and sacred life truly is.

From this vision we can understand the pattern of change that must come. We must begin to share the world's wealth rather than continue to exploit it on an ever-increasing scale. The American empire alone controls an estimated 40 percent of the world's wealth, while its people comprise only 6 percent of the global population. As America and other highly developed technological nations move through the twentieth century, the other two-thirds of the world lie in crowded and rapidly deteriorating conditions symptomatic of the perilous Dark Ages.

International cooperation and planning aimed at creating a just world economic order, halting the perilous spread of nuclear capability to other nations, and building mutual and lasting alliances in the fields of population growth, ecological deterioration, and economic development are crucial for our future survival and peace. In my view, this can best occur within the framework of a two-tiered political structure in the world: above, a globalization of world political communities, extending international agreements and law, and, below, a decentralized structure which could, if adopted by nations, serve to implement these agreements at the lowest and most efficient level.

The technological method, which has freed humanity in so many ways, can be maintained; but the growing complex of blind economic power that controls the lives of so many must be reduced in size and given human terms again. As with small-scale political organizations, simpler technologies that directly serve the individual communities in this country and elsewhere around the world should be fostered. This would dramatically decrease the dependence of humankind on the economic manipulations of national and international corporations. We must allow for the redivision and extension

of economic ownership before the power of such concentrated wealth is so closely guarded that it is unable to be
broken. As Schumacher tells us:

> The cultivation and expansion of needs is the antithesis of
> wisdom. It is also the antithesis of freedom and peace. Every
> increase of needs tends to increase one's dependence on outside
> forces over which one cannot have control, and therefore
> increases existential fear. Only by a reduction of needs can one
> promote a genuine reduction in those tensions which are the
> ultimate causes of strife and war.[9]

Facing our fears and ourselves may well be a dangerous
undertaking, but it is what is needed to allow us, as a nation
and a world, to live on. The scale of the task before us might
easily be frightening, for it requires a deep spiritual battle
with the truth.

We must, as Thomas Merton suggests, acknowledge that
we *all* have more or less been wrong, that we *all* are at fault,
all limited and obstructed by our mixed motives, our self-
deception, our greed, our self-righteousness and our tendency
to aggressiveness and hypocrisy.

Rediscovering the past and reenvisioning the future begins
with each of us, in the search for our souls. Liberation is a
profoundly spiritual task requiring us to discover interior
resources that have, for so long, lain dormant. Only from
such an inward journey can we hope to build the internal
energy and courage that enable us to confront life in this
modern age and act to reshape the contours of humanity's
corporate life. Such moral and spiritual liberation can free
us to love those whom we fear and to understand that they
are our hope, just as we are theirs. As Merton continues:

> [We] can learn to love them even in their sin, as God has
> loved them. If we can love the men we cannot trust and if we
> can to some extent share the burden of their sin by identifying
> ourselves with them, then perhaps there is some hope of a kind
> of peace on earth, based not on the wisdom and the manipula-
> tions of men but on the inscrutable mercy of God. For only

love—which means humility—can exorcise the fear which is at the root of all war.

　　Love other men and love God above all. And instead of hating the people you think are warmakers, hate the appetites and the disorder in your own soul, which are the causes of war. If you love peace, then hate injustice, hate tyranny, hate greed—but hate these things in yourself, not in another.[10]

It is not, then, through a sense of bland optimism, nor of blind pessimism, that we should understand human destiny. It is rather through a depth of endurance found in the human soul—a sense of struggle and inner purpose that bore the Christians through the persecutions of early Rome, a nation through its birthpangs two hundred years ago, and the Jews through the human wasteland of Dachau, Auschwitz, and the other death camps of the Third Reich.

What matters in the end, it seems to me, is the vision which we each hold in our hearts. That is based, in turn, on what we ultimately believe about our existence in the world. If we believe that the basis of life is a spiritual one, grounded in a loving God, then we will nourish a hope for our future that rests upon his faithfulness as the sacrificial lover of a lost world. We act then, on faith—not with the certain knowledge that our deeds will alter history's course, but with the inner assurance that holding forth such a faith is the first and most important act required of us.

I have found the focus of my faith to rest on Jesus of Nazareth, who said he came as the full revelation of God's truth and life. That has come through a long personal, spiritual journey. And it is he who gives me my basis for charting life and for hoping in a future based upon revolutionary spiritual values.

If humanity is to emerge with any promise into the next century, we must unlock all our spiritual resources. Without them, I believe that we will either destroy ourselves, or be destroyed by our hatreds and greeds.

When we docked at Hiroshima many of the navy men aboard my vessel saw immediately the scarcity of food among the Japanese. Most were drawn to give their lunches to the frightened, hungry children of Hiroshima. Suddenly we were sharing food with people who had been our arch-enemies a few weeks before. Amidst the rubble of a nuclear bomb, even while bodies were being pillaged, that simple act of communion in the wake of such unspeakable evil seemed to be a small redeeming sign of hope.

Chapter 11

A
Liberating
Revolution

TWO HUNDRED years ago, the American Revolution was attempting to sweep away the vestiges of political power practiced without equal political representation. The fight for liberty on this continent had begun. It was a struggle that Jefferson believed must have no end; he believed other revolutions might be required about every twenty-five years.

The birth of America tore away at the traditions of tyranny that had characterized so much of civilization. The barefoot, hungry armies of George Washington fought for the overriding primacy of one concept—the right of any individual to be free from the coercion of abusive and freedom-destroying power. The struggles of those years were toward human liberation. The beginning of the American experiment was for many throughout the world a breath of fresh life for humanity's purpose and dignity. History was challenged, and changed.

What, then, have we become since the Revolution? In 1776 we were a nation of small political and economic units based on agrarianism. But during the course of two centuries the traditional way of American life has been stretched to accommodate the dynamism of superindustrialism, and we have experienced a vast centralization of economic and political power. This, along with a number of other cultural changes, has caused dramatic population shifts from countryside to city. It has given rise to massive industry which requires the availability of a huge labor force and abundant, cheap raw materials; it has caused the mechanization of society; it has spawned the multinational corporation and the economic cartel; and it has created an intricate and highly centralized form of government to deal with the growth of the industrialism and the problems of a democracy in a modern, technologically dominated age.

What are the parameters of governmental power? Between 1930 and 1974 the gross national product (GNP) increased 15 times—from $90.4 billion to $1.4 trillion. During the same period federal expenditures increased over 106 times—from $2.8 billion to $298 billion, or seven times faster than the increase in GNP. Federal tax receipts have increased 97 times—from $3 billion to $291 billion in that same period of 44 years. This is over six times as fast as the increase in GNP.

Other statistics provide ample evidence of the growing bureaucratization of American democracy. One out of every six American workers is now employed by federal, state, or local government. There are currently 14.5 million civilian workers on the public payroll receiving $42 billion in salaries, fringe benefits and allowances. Not including the armed forces, there are 2.9 million federal employees alone, almost equaling in number the American colonists who rebelled against their king 200 years ago.

We are, then, a culture of vast political dimensions, the dynamics of which bear little resemblance to the traditions of the past. The New England town meeting, where citizens gathered in small groups to determine appropriate action on matters affecting the community as a whole, has been replaced by the political party, the city machine, and pluralism on a massive scale in which powerful interest groups vie for the accommodation of their government.

We seem bound by the power of government to corporate and political structures which serve more and more to regulate our lives and detract from our liberties.

During the early years of this century, the Austrian novelist and poet Franz Kafka wrote a startling and nightmarish story called "The Castle." In it Kafka, like so many novelists of the modern age, paints a frightening picture of a separate world and a separate social order in which the people completely abandon their freedom and initiative in fear of those who rule their lives.

The story centers on one Mr. K., a land surveyor who has been hired by rulers of the Castle. The reasons for his hiring are unknown to everyone, including Mr. K. Upon arrival at the designated area, a confused Mr. K. goes to great lengths in an effort to clarify his position. What is his purpose? Why has he been summoned? Everyone he meets tells him that there is, unfortunately, no need at all for a land surveyor. In fact, they cannot explain the reasons for his presence.

Mr. K. makes every effort to establish a rationale for his existence. He confronts authority figures with no success. He is only told: "You haven't once come in contact with our real authorities. All these contacts are merely illusory, but owing to your ignorance . . . you take them to be real."

Somewhat like a trained house pet, Mr. K. does not leave. Authority has summoned him and despite the clear indication that no purpose whatever exists in his being there, he remains. He accomplishes nothing. His time is consumed in trying to search out someone who will tell him what to do and how to proceed. It is time wasted, for Mr. K. is lost in a world of unseen power. He is controlled by a person or persons he has neither seen nor met.

Finally, Mr. K. receives a letter from the Castle. The message of authority reads as follows: "The surveying work which you have carried out thus far has my recognition.

. . . Do not slacken your efforts. Bring your work to a successful conclusion. Any interruption would displease me.
. . . I shall not forget you."

As Mr. K.'s confusion clears, if only temporarily, Kafka's
point is made. The purpose of Mr. K. is, simply, to have
no purpose. He exists only to be controlled. This is the
dictate of the State and Mr. K., with no options and no will
of his own, must accept the ruling.

Although "The Castle" is a world located only in the
visions of Kafka's mind, I believe its tale of alienation and
authoritarian oppression offers insight into the culture and
dangers in the civilization of twentieth-century America. As
with Kafka's world, we have become a people whose freedoms
are slowly being suffocated by organizations and institutions,
both political and economic, beyond our power to control.
Faced with massive challenges to our nation in this century,
we have created systems, techniques, industrial design, and
political apparatus on a scale large enough to deal with
them. In turn, we have experienced an era of unparalleled
prosperity. Yet, we have also a technical culture which, in
many ways, serves to diminish the importance and freedom
of humanity.

Some sociologists have noted that genuine social life, and
traditional cultural bonds, are constantly being fractured by
twentieth-century urban and industrial pressures. Genuine
social order, stressing the cohesion of community, family, and
religion, has become obsolete, they say. Even in the nineteenth century, Emile Durkheim observed that society had become a "disorganized dust of individuals," held precariously
together by the imposition of political power.

In the twentieth century, modern technology and the
necessities of industrial life have brought us mobility; but
they have created a transient society where interpersonal
relationships are established, broken, and reestablished in
an endless succession of change. The case of Lima, Peru,
dramatically illustrates this cultural trend.

During the 1920s, Lima had a population of 175,000. In
five decades, the population increased seventeen times until
today it holds three million people. This migration from

the rural hinterlands to the metropolitan core occurred, as
with most cities in the industrial era, without structure and
without control. E. F. Shumacher indicates what has resulted:

> The once beautiful Spanish city is now infested by slums,
> surrounded by misery-belts that are crawling up the Andes.
> But this is not all. People are arriving from the rural areas at
> the rate of a thousand a day—and nobody knows what to do
> with them. The social or psychological structure of life in the
> hinterland has collapsed; people are becoming foot loose and
> arrive in the capital city at the rate of a thousand a day to
> squat on some empty land, against the police who come to
> beat them out, to build their mud hovels and look for a job.
> And nobody knows what to do about them. Nobody knows
> how to stop the drift.[1]

Undeniably, the symptoms of social disintegration are different in the superindustrialized countries of the western
world. But they are surely there, and they grow worse, even
as our centralized system of government attempts, often
vainly, to deal with the causes of cultural and social breakdown.

The sense of loss in which these symptoms are measured
can be seen in the growth in suicide, and in the number of
our young who have chosen to live in complete isolation from
urbanized, industrialized life. The symptoms are witnessed
in feelings of alienation in modern humanity—alienation
from work, from community, from government, and often,
from ourselves. Ironically, these feelings are deeply rooted in
the fear, apathy and hatred caused by growing spiritual and
psychological dissatisfaction amid the greatest material splendor in the history of human development. Such symptoms
of inner estrangement are present in us all and, taken together, they constitute a sense of corporate alienation from
twentieth-century life.

In a conscientious effort to deal with the critical problems
caused by the industrial revolution, government, as we have
seen, has experienced quantum growth. In order to initiate
the great programs of our past—the New Deals, the Great
Societies, the Wars on Poverty, and the New Federalisms—

it was necessary, we believed, to co-opt individual and community responsibility through the creation of centralized, federal bureaucracies. Officials proceeded on the assumption that these great citadels of paper and people would provide the most practical way of overcoming the problems of welfare for the disadvantaged, inadequate housing, economic opportunity for the unemployed, and a fair distribution of wealth.

As we view the effect of government on modern humanity, we can see that many of these assumptions have proven wrong, and should be challenged. Nevertheless, we are left with the monolithic dinosaurs of those misconceptions, huge buildings lining the streets of Washington whose inhabitants attempt to carry out the nation's business.

The bureaucracy, by virtue of the direction it has been given in past decades, deals fundamentally with external conditions of American civilization. It issues general declarations that affect us all in very specific and very different ways. It cannot, through such generalities, address itself effectively to the distinctiveness of communities, or the separateness of problems that may exist in one manner in Brooklyn, New York, and in quite another manner in Eugene, Oregon. The bureaucracy, in an effort to maintain responsible national policies, must homogenize the distinctions among individuals and in all communities, no matter how varied the experience of each may be. This may be a failure of good intention, but the intention itself has now been bespoiled.

If a welfare program is administered poorly and is, then, abused by those not in desperate need of basic assistance, welfare as a charitable and necessary function of a wealthy society is demeaned and castigated by people as being merely a "giveaway" to hustlers, prostitutes, and the lazy. The essential purpose of welfare, to provide economic assistance to those who cannot otherwise live decent lives, is lost in the sarcasm of the age.

The sense of frustration among our people engendered by failure of this type cannot be computed, but it can be sensed. I need only ask my constituents if they think government can solve their problems. Most all think not.

People believe the federal government has grown too big; that it spends far too much money to accomplish far too little; that what it does spend it frequently wastes; that it has lost touch with the citizens; that it employs too many presumptuous bureaucrats; and that it blunders on, not in control of itself, nor controlled by others. To an unsettling degree, they are right.

In both business and government one of the most historically significant phenomena has been the massive growth of bureaucracy. Bureaucrats become specialists in a specialized age. They dictate policy and they hold real power. They are not elected to their positions; yet their decisions are far-reaching, affecting millions of lives daily in both the political and economic spheres of influence.

They must, because of the remoteness of their position, treat the people over whose lives they exercise control as objects to be manipulated for the soundest and most efficient means toward achieving a goal. The goals can be very different—from increasing production capacity by offering incentives to factory workers, to decreasing the number of people illegally receiving food stamps by creating additional regulations. In each case, however, the bureaucrat comes to view those under his or her control with dispassionate reason and an absence of feeling. Most certainly, this adds to the alienation in both citizens and workers who feel their lives are being dictated by forces beyond their power to control.

Spawned by institutionalized bureaucracy, this alienation is in large part a function of the massive size of society's corporate and political apparatus. It is perpetuated by an unwillingness toward change, a resistance to chart any new course for government or for work that is a fundamental alternative to the complex centralization of modern institutions. Continued estrangement is a result of a failure of imagination, and a sullen complacency regarding the institutions that surround us. Society rewards those who "do not make waves" and whose answer to every question of purpose is: "I do not make the rules. I am merely administering them."

The growth of both big business and government continues unabated. Thomas Jefferson understood the dangers in such concentration of wealth and such control over people's lives. He believed that a healthy American democracy rested heavily on the existence of large numbers of small property owners and farmers. Thus, Americans could stand up to government and economic tyranny without fear of deprivation. They could be free from the bonds of economic and political necessity that endangered individual liberty.

Who owns wealth today? Corporations account for 56 percent of our nation's economic income of wealth. The largest 100 firms directly control about 50 percent of all industrial assets. This represents more control than was held by the 200 major corporations twenty-five years ago. Today's 200 largest firms control about two-thirds of industrial assets, or roughly equivalent to the percentage controlled by the 1,000 largest firms at the outbreak of World War II. In 1921 there were no less than 88 auto manufacturers in the United States. That number has now been reduced essentially to three. In 1975, these three companies produced 97 percent of all domestic cars sold in the country.

The incorporation of American capitalism has proceeded rapidly, despite legal efforts to restrain that influence in our national economy and over the lives of working people. Huge farms, corporately owned, push the individual farmer from his land, which becomes part of the corporate whole. Food chains create the "supermarket," and the neighborhood store is forced into bankruptcy.

Corporate America controls millions of lives, eight hours a day, for the great span of each person's life. People in the modern, superindustrial age work together, accomplishing rapidly and efficiently the creation of a singular product, but they no longer work for themselves. They labor for a frequently unseen and economically powerful entity, the corporation. They are a specialized people; they often do not even see the final product of their efforts. Although strides have been made in some corporations in recent years to adjust working conditions to prevent monotony and a sense of robotism among corporate workers, the purpose of their labor is bereft of personal meaning. This situation, Erich Fromm says, makes "machines which act like men and produces men who act like machines."[2]

In terms of historical, human freedoms, what does this centralization of power mean? For the most part, it means the replacement of originality and initiative with a mindless compliance to the corporate system and to managerial experts who run it. In a very real sense, corporate industrialism is homogenizing the distinction of the millions of workers who sustain it. Lives become dedicated, in mass, to the acquisition of material wealth. The shape of capitalism is changed, and the effect of capitalism on democracy is altered, reflecting the power of mass industrialism.

The corporate worker often lives in the suburbs, commuting daily to his work, fulfilling his specified purpose for a specified period of time, returning home at the usual hour, only to begin the ritual again the next day. The deep individual need for self-fulfillment is abandoned by the design of the assembly line, the managerial stopwatch, and finally by the worker. No matter how great the material benefits, the union laborer who attaches tens of thousands of windshield wipers to assembly-line cars for forty years does not represent the substance of the American dream that Jefferson and others conceived.

Such a growing emotional dependence on both corporate and political bigness is leading our civilization in new, dramatic directions. Institutional authority forms its own silent tyrannies, which, in turn, erode democracy and the principles of genuine liberty.

Central problems to be resolved within the cultural parameters of twentieth-century life are those of relevancy, of size, of human liberation from institutional oppression, and of the restoration of community. If the threat of nuclear war constitutes the preeminent danger to the continued existence of civilization, so the threat of de facto bureaucratic power poses the gravest dangers to the worth of life within the confines of that civilization.

Estrangement and alienation, the emotional by-products of superindustrialism, have crippled a people who desire to be free.

What is the alternative to the massive growth of both industry and State? I believe it lies, simply and logically, in smallness, through decentralization. It is essential that the processes, within both the political and economic spheres, be returned to dimensions that can be affected and molded by the people who now live their lives under the unswerving influence of centralization.

This must, in the political world, take the form of a massive and legitimate return of power to the citizens of this nation. Such a dramatic decentralization of power, which could be accomplished within the existing structures of the federal, state and local government, could help rekindle the spirit which lay at the heart of the American Revolution. This is a spirit which we must find again if we are to ensure that our democratic liberties are to have any authentic meaning in our third century of existence as a nation.

The mechanism, nationwide, that can be used for such purpose would center in the establishment of neighborhood and community governments. Such small-sized organizations, simple in design and yet effective in the reestablishment of true participatory democracy, could revitalize the spirit of America. As they grew in strength and relevance, the scope of the federal government would diminish.

Moreover, these neighborhood governments should be granted real, not circumspect, power. Each member of a neighborhood organization for self-government should be able to receive a tax credit of up to 80 percent of his or her federal income tax payment by channeling it directly into such an organization, in lieu of giving it to Washington. Face-to-face groups could then debate and act with their own resources to solve the problems directly affecting the life of their community.

Neighborhood government is an alternative that could begin the restoration of liberty, dignity, and true democracy to towns, city-neighborhoods, and communities—the heartland of America. And the return of political power to people who would choose to take it is not a gift from Congress or from the federal government; it is a right which forms the foundation of our Constitution.

Local day-care centers, drug-abuse centers, halfway houses, and outpatient health clinics can be established to meet specific community needs. Parks and recreation centers, welfare programs, cooperative stores, banks and credit unions, and local police forces and fire departments, all meeting established standards, are all possible if the people that comprise community and city neighborhoods are given direct control of tax monies that are so often wasted.

These neighborhoods should have some right and power to decide where a city's freeways are built. Local communities in the midst of urban sprawl must assume the power to determine how their land should be utilized, and how their ecology should be protected. Towns should give their citizens the option of choosing whether industries that would cause pollution or manufacture unwanted products should be allowed to reside there. Also, localized, decentralized government must assume responsibility of caring for the dispossessed, and meeting the social needs left unfulfilled by the imposition of federal directives and by federal monies that often prove insufficient.

There is nothing more American than community-based self-government in which people can deal with their own problems and resources. The town meeting, the voluntary organizations, the P.T.A., and the neighborhood associations have been historic, tangible expressions of self-determination and liberty.

The movement toward a fundamental decentralization of institutional power will no doubt begin quietly, with existing, highly developed neighborhood associations comprising the vanguard. With success, it will grow to allow the voices of all Americans to be heard—and what is said will make a difference. No longer will their cries fall on the deaf ears of a massive and plodding federal bureaucracy that cannot feel their pain, sense their hunger, or offer them hope.

The movement back to communities has begun. The Sto-Rox Community near Pittsburgh, working with little or no outside federal assistance and against entrenched political machinery, has incorporated itself and become a viable expression of grass-roots community self-government. The citizens of Sto-Rox have established a community health center, a senior citizens clinic, a library and a counseling center. It serves the community well because the people know the community problems firsthand and have set about to cure them.

In Washington, D.C., the Adams Morgan Organization is in the process of developing community self-sufficiency both politically and economically. In addition to the neighborhood assembly which meets regularly to discuss and solve community problems, citizens have established a community technology center which plans fish tanks to be placed in the basements of neighborhood homes, each of which might be able to produce 400 pounds of rainbow trout a month. Hydroponic greenhouses that could be community-owned and operated have been proposed; they would be placed on the roofs of downtown buildings and homes, and it is estimated that they could provide the food needs of every member of the neighborhood at extraordinarily cheap prices. In addition, plans have been created for harnessing wind and solar energy to run the kitchens and heat the water of neighborhood homes. This is an effort to make communities as economically independent as possible from energy sources dependent on national and international circumstances beyond their direct power to control.

These are only a few examples of a quiet movement that is occurring throughout this nation today amid the frenzy of our superindustrial age. Innovative neighborhood corporations individually and collectively are exercising their liberty, rather than having it decay and erode under the benign despotism of institutional centralized government. Confronting human problems in human terms, they are succeeding in the battle because they have imagination and compassion.

With an emphasis on smallness and political manageability, politics in the future could anticipate change rather than become a victim of it. Politics would be an integral part of the neighborhoods and communities of America, where the need for change is first felt. People able to stand up, speak their minds and be heard can bring about immediate political action. In community debate, whether it be on the qualities of a Presidential candidate, or the need for street and sidewalk repair, I anticipate much waving of hands, many shouts to be heard and a great deal of carrying on. I welcome all these things, for they are the sounds of people acting together again, sounds of life and political rebirth. They are what is needed to cope with an increasingly complex future, and to energize anew the American political experience.

An equally dramatic decentralization of our corporate economic life must accompany such political decentralization. True liberation and freedom will be possible only if both the political and economic centralization of our society are replaced by fundamental viable alternatives.

As through the ages, work dominates our daily existence. But, as we have seen, the character of work has altered as rapidly as our American culture. Where before work was arduous, tied to the land and to the rigors of climate and nature, work now occurs in predetermined, eight-hour cycles, often in air-conditioned comfort, and in wholly predictable and computed patterns.

It is dominated by the machine, by managerial bureaucracy, and by the sheer size of the organization for which a person labors. Before a person's work required a presence— a direct involvement characterized by varied decisions critical to the ultimate success of one's labors: when to plant, how to recover crops from an unpredicted storm, how to encircle and kill faster prey, where to build a neighborhood store, or to repair handmade tools. Work now limits personal involvement and individual accomplishment to conditioned, automatic responses, and a programmed lack of creativity.

If modern humanity is not to lose its finest qualities to the techniques of industrialism, the inner function of industrialism itself should be changed, and dramatically so. The benefits to humanity which have come from industrialization we should retain, of course. But within the corporate world, as with big government, there should begin a concentrated effort toward decentralization and smallness.

Smallness, in this sense, not only implies a breakdown of the intrastructure of the corporation into smaller operating units, but also a recognition within those units of the individual needs and aspirations of the worker. These could entail such variables as employee stock-ownership plans, in which the worker has a fundamental interest in the success of the company as a whole; worker information periods, in which the laborer joins with others in his or her group, on company time, in an information discussion concerning the total function of the plant or office, and what part the individual's position plays in the whole project; counseling services for the worker to discover possible discontent so that solutions may be realized; and worker representation on the board of directors of corporations as liaison to explain the direction of the organization at meetings, and in turn, relay the thoughts of worker teams directly to the board.

The organization should, above all else, remain receptive to change. Rather than dictating policy from above, change should emanate from the working force. Workers should be intricately involved in the process of the corporation so that they will be aware of the negative and positive effect every decision will have on their circumstances.

Superindustrialism and the advent of national and multinational corporations impose, by their nature, enormous economic pressure on smaller operations. The rapid incorporation of American industrial assets in the last decades can only mean the certain elimination of small business in coming decades, if adequate safeguards are not written into law and applied strenuously. Thus, incentives should be given to promote new, smaller entrepreneurship.

So long as industrialism continues to advance worldwide, it is incumbent that we commit ourselves not to blind materialistic growth, but to individual fulfillment. Society cannot exist without order, but neither can it grow strong and vital without the allowance for the growth of individuality. As we have led the industrial revolution, so must we take the leadership in insuring that industrialism does not become an *end* in itself, with human beings constituting the *means* toward that achievement. As superindustrialism extends toward the more remote corners of the world, threatening to change the lives of others as it changed our own, we must remember that it must exist for humanity's benefit; we must not exist for it. If we cannot begin to place all human beings, bureaucrat and Senator, citizen and worker, above the goals of materialism, there seems little hope for the world culture as we approach the twenty-first century.

The great Russian novelist Tolstoy warned early in this century:

> The medieval theology, or the Roman corruption of morals, poisoned only their own people, a small part of mankind; today, electricity, railways and telegraphs spoil the whole world. Everyone makes these things his own. He simply cannot help making his own. Everyone suffering in the same way, is forced to the same extent to change his way of life. All are under the necessity of betraying what is most important for their lives, the understanding of life itself, religion. Machines—to produce what? The telegraph—to dispatch what? Books, papers—to spread what kind of news? Railways—to go to whom and to what place? Millions of people herded together to and subject to a supreme power—to accomplish what? [3]

These questions remain unanswered, but the technological, industrial and institutional power that provoked Tolstoy's concern has come to form one foundation of modern life. Through misuse that power, corporate and political, can become anathema to human dignity, freedom and liberation.

So it was with the lost souls in Kafka's authoritarian world. Somewhere, sometime—Kafka will not tell us exactly when—tyranny grew; and liberty, humanity, and, finally, civilized culture were destroyed.

With Kafka tyranny was not overt; it did not take the form of a screaming madman appealing only to the weakest traits in people. Tyranny was subtle, silent, persuasive, and yet still as deadly. And so it is today.

The quantum growth of institutional power in the industrial age has bred a strange, despondent alienation among those who live by its sufferance. Such alienation threatens to breed, in turn, the tyranny of authoritarianism.

In Kafka's world the individual became a machine. Devoid of will, he was a passionless, joyless servant of authority and control. Mr. K. was as emotionally dead as the rulers who governed his life, and he symbolized a society which had little future, and no purpose.

In our own society, alienation, apathy and confusion exist to an unsettling degree, posing a major danger to the historic foundations of democracy. Centralization of work and State, with the quiet precision of a computer, has already begun to undermine our freedoms and is monotonously and systematically destroying our spirit.

We must stop this massive trend. We cannot live with dignity as nameless servants to institutions that may grow so large as to be beyond our ability to control. Rather, we must build new, decentralized structures for political and economic life, enabling the rebirth of opportunity for creativity, liberty, true community, and purpose in life.

As our nation moves into its third century, we find ourselves strangely spiritless at a time when we desperately need renewed spirit for looking forward. The Church here again has a unique role to play, for the estrangement experienced by modern humanity flows fundamentally from the loss of true community. That is what the band of those committed to the Good News can restore. A beginning point for their witness is the setting forth of a model for community which rests on new values and embodies the first signs of a New Order in the world. Economically, socially, racially, and spiritually, such new communities can point the way to the rest of the world, and become true means of hope for us all to build a future of promise and creativity.

Chapter 12

Stewards
of Creation

I ENJOY many external things about Washington,
D.C. It is blessed with beautiful works of nature and of
architectural grandeur. A walk through the Capitol, the
White House, or the various memorials plunges one into a
wealth of past history.

But there is another place which is infinitely closer to my
heart. It's not a marble shrine, nor a place which attracts
millions of visitors. In fact, if it did I would not feel toward
it as I do. That special place is atop a 100-foot cliff overlooking the Oregon Pacific coastline. At high tide the ocean
lashes against the cliff. Extending westward is a rocky point
at the end of which is the Yaquina Head lighthouse. On a
clear night a great arc of light floods out from the lighthouse
and briefly illuminates the sea and the darkness that does
not seem to end.

In this setting of gnarled pine, spruce, cedar, and fir that grow along this magnificent section of the Oregon coast is an old weather-beaten stump that I enjoy sitting on as I overlook the vast stretch of sand and the ocean beyond. For it is there that I really feel I have the time and seclusion needed to develop a perspective on the actions in which I am involved. That is precisely why this place is so special to me; it is for reflection, for contemplation. I believe that it cannot be quite as special for anyone else, for its uniqueness is related to my experience each time I visit that point.

As I sit on that common old stump and simply sense the might of the ocean, my heart is directed to worship. Affairs of the political world seem so temporary in the light of God's creation, and I realize that Washington, D.C., really is not so powerful or significant in his divine scheme. These times of reflection help me deal with the common temptation to exalt ego, for the vastness of creation quietly humbles one's spirit.

What majesty lies before us in the created world. I can only join the Psalmist in pondering, "What is man that thou art mindful of him?" (8:4). And what trust our Creator has placed in us. In the same Psalm, David utters amazement that God has "given him [humanity] dominion over the works of [God's] hands."

What have we done with this trust? Some would point to the technological advancements of recent years and say that we are approaching utopia, nearly in control of our environment, and our future. We can encourage and prevent birth, we can eliminate disease, and we can develop power from the smallest building block of the universe, the atom.

But in what we have called "progress," we have misunderstood the intended relationship which we are to have with the earth itself. Our quest has been self-centered. We have only partially obeyed the command in Genesis 1:28, and that obedience has not been intentional, I suspect. Yes, we have been fruitful and we have multiplied. We have developed dominion over the fish of the sea and over the animals of the earth. We have subdued the earth. But we have not replenished it. We have not cared for that which we hold in trust.

Two impressive studies—a scientific experiment with mice and an anthropological study from Africa—have direct relevance on our situation in America today, I believe, and reflect our broken relationship with our created world.

Dr. John Calhoun, a research psychologist at the National Institute of Mental Health, built a nine-foot square cage for selected mice and observed them as their population grew from 8 to 2,200. The cage was designed to contain comfortably a population of 160. Food, water, and other resources were always abundant. All the mortality factors except aging were eliminated. As the population reached its peak at 2,200 after about two and one-half years, the colony of mice began to disintegrate. There was no physical escape from their closed environment. Adults formed natural groups of about a dozen individual mice. In the groups each mouse performed a particular social role, but there were no roles in which to place the healthy young mice. This totally disrupted the whole society. The males who had protected their territory withdrew from leadership. The females became aggressive and forced out the young. And the young grew to be only self-indulgent. They ate, drank, slept, groomed themselves, but showed no normal aggression and failed to reproduce.

Dr. Calhoun observed that courtship and mating—the most complex activities for mice—were the first activities to cease. After five years all of the mice had died, despite the fact that they had plenty of water, food, and no disease. What result would such overcrowding have on humanity? Dr. Calhoun suggests that we would first of all cease to reproduce our ideas, and along with ideas, our goals and ideals. In other words, our values would be lost.[1]

The second study which I think is very pertinent also is that of the IK society. I know of few examples that have had more relevance to theories of modern life than the experiences of the IK. Dr. Colin Turnbull studied the IK society near the upper tributaries of the White Nile River in Africa. From his observations came the book *The Mountain People*.[2]

Until twenty-five to thirty years ago, the IK were a hunting people. As with the American Indian, theirs was a true conservation ethic. Overhunting was a great sin in their society. Using bows, nets, and pitfalls in their hunting, they maintained a cooperative spirit with their environment. Traditions, rituals, beliefs, and values molded and preserved a continuity of life. When the government of Uganda decided to make the main hunting ground of the IK a national park, however, hunting in their valley became forbidden. The IK, forced to move, were encouraged to become farmers. Whereas they had previously roamed through a large valley, the IK were now crowded together into a confined area. The result of these actions was a reversal of the cooperative and humanitarian spirit that had characterized these people.

The great tribal hunts were over and solitary hunting was necessary for survival. Sharing food, even with family members, ceased, and withholding it became an accomplishment. The IK lived in crowded groups characterized by hostility and loneliness, laughing only at the mistakes of others. One mentally afflicted girl whom Turnbull observed believed that food should be shared and that parents were to be loved and to love. She was beaten by her peers and locked in her hut by her parents until she died.

Just as the mice had ceased to live as mice, the IK ceased to live as people and lost their compassion. Why? The resulting shift from a mobile hunter-gatherer way of life to stable agrarian life made all the rituals, traditions, beliefs, and values irrelevant. Further, the IK were suddenly crowded together with a density, intimacy, and frequency of contact far greater than they had ever been required to experience.

The danger of altering the environment in which we exist to the extent that our deepest values are not only neglected but lost now threatens our civilization. Obvious evidence is the population concentration in our twentieth-century culture called the megalopolis. In the brief period of time from 1950 to the present, population concentration in our metropolitan areas has risen from 56 percent to 69 percent of our total population. In 1970, the census indicated that three-fourths of our population growth in the last ten years has been in the metropolitan areas; by the end of the century, the experts project that 100 million Americans (a number equal to the combined population of Britain and France) will be added to our population. Over three-quarters of the 300 million Americans will be concentrated in major urban areas if the present trend continues.

There are very obvious results from this kind of concentration. Consider New York City. A person in a typical midtown Manhattan office works within ten minutes of 220,000 people. In a typical, moderately sized American city, an individual works within ten minutes of 20,000 people, while in a suburb the number would be about 11,000 people.

All the normal problems that exist in any community are intensified by the increase of population density—pollution, transportation, waste disposal, crime, housing, and energy supply. Any of the national, state, or local issues today are but compounded by this kind of population concentration. There is also a deeper social and psychological effect in the erosion of trust between people and the impersonality that develops in human relationships. Ironically, the emotional condition of the "sexually liberated" was described in the *Washingtonian* magazine as a "fear of feeling."

In a study recently conducted by the City University of New York, individuals were sent out from the University to various homes and apartments in New York City. Appearing at the door as strangers, they knocked or rang the bell and asked to use the phone, saying that they had misplaced a telephone number of a friend they were seeking to visit. These same individuals were then sent out from New York City into several small towns and villages. You can guess the results. The individuals were between two and five times more likely to be invited into the house in the smaller towns than in the city. The Good Samaritan impulse and the willingness of people to be responsible for the well-being of others seems to be reduced in proportion to the increase in the number of people in a given area. Overconcentration results in actions that cause fear, thus isolating people from one another.

The larger and more concentrated our cities become, the more isolated individuals become. With that isolation comes a dependence upon government to provide more services. Government is asked to curb crime, and to provide for the poor, the elderly, and the infirm. These are legitimate requests, but the larger a city grows, the more difficult it becomes to govern.

In all of this, our sense of community has been eroded. Consider the town of Roseto, Pennsylvania. Roseto was a small Italian-American community of about 1,600 people. In 1961, it became known as a "miracle town" when medical researchers discovered that in this little community no one under fifty had suffered a fatal heart attack. Records going back to 1955 indicated that heart-attack fatalities among older people were far below the national average. Ten years later the researchers returned and found that two men in their early forties had died of heart attacks that year, and that the overall rate of heart attack fatalities had been rising sharply over a period of several years. Why? The study showed that over the decade, life-styles began changing in Roseto. The close-knit family relationships, with men working in the quarries and the women in the blouse mills, no longer were the norm. To get better-paying jobs the men began to commute twenty to thirty miles away from their town. They began buying new things and sending their children away to colleges. Worries multiplied and individual competition replaced cooperation. Food became richer in cost and in cholesterol. One medical researcher concluded that the people of Roseto became "Americanized." The local pastor put it another way: "We have joined the rat race." [3]

I am not suggesting that we should dismiss concerns about the advantages of education or all other material goals and benefits. I am only indicating some of the by-products of the cultural values that have become the national norm. These values, reflected in our concern for an ever-larger gross national product and our consumer-oriented economy, have engendered enormous psychological pressures in modern America far beyond the power and scope of government fundamentally to alter. We have previously noted the increasing toll that the patterns of contemporary living are taking in the lives of Americans in terms of growth of depression and mental illness, in the alienation of workers from their jobs, and in general from the enlarged sense of corporate anxiety and lack of meaning in life.

What do we conclude from the mice, the IK and these other observations and studies? Human beings need space— physical and mental space, territory in which to live and think. But let me add another conclusion which is often overlooked. All people are in desperate need of caring relationships, and communities of compassion. We need values that nurture liability for the fulfillment and needs of others. And we must no longer look merely to government to do it for us. Government is at best a method. What we face, here again, is a spiritual task. Leadership marked by a unique sensitivity to the needs of the total person is required.

Christian faith proclaims Good News for the whole person, not just for the soul or just for the body. The message of redemption is made manifest in corporate life, not just in individuals. The presence of committed Christians should be one of redemptive influence, with concern for the whole person—the spiritual, temporal, and material needs of all.

It must be the responsibility of the Christian community to reestablish in our society a model of people who know how to care for each other and an ethic which reaches out to the world at large with this sensitivity and commitment. Christians are uniquely suited to the task, for not only do we have the motivating command of Christ to love one another, but we also are promised the transcendent power to do so.

Our responsibility does not stop with the spiritual or even with the relational aspects of Christianity. If that were so we would be overlooking a major element influencing humanity's condition—God's call to the stewardship of our environment. The world is ultimately God's good creation. Although the whole of creation has suffered the consequences of sin, we are not free to disregard the physical world in which we live. We are caretakers, not exploiters. Only as we assume the responsibility to care for the physical world will we be ministering to the whole person. Humanity cannot be separated from its environment.

Dr. Max Kaplan, director of the University of South Florida's leisure studies program, has found that the normal extension of automation has reduced the work week roughly from 70 to 37 hours in the past century, almost four hours per week less by the decade. This rate will be intensified by five hours in the '70s, six hours in the '80s, and seven hours in the '90s. The result would be a work week of twenty hours by the year 2000. More and more people are taking early retirement, in both civilian and military life. The University of Oregon's Institute of Industrial and Labor Relations found that three-fourths of West Coast retirees voluntarily decided on early retirement. Seventy percent agreed that they wanted to stop working so they could enjoy retired life.[4]

The obvious question, then, is "Will we be prepared to use all this time?" In my opinion, this relates along with other factors directly to our relationship with our environment.

How we use our land is one of the more critical factors in the future of our society. Of the approximately 2,266,-000,000 acres of land in the United States, 1 percent provides living space for people; about 28 percent is used for grazing livestock; 20 percent to grow food; 1 percent for transportation; 6 percent for recreation; and 33 percent for forestry. The other 11 percent is used for other purposes. How the patterns of our society develop in the future will be determined in large measure by the manner in which this land is used. Where will people live? How dispersed or concentrated will the population be? Where should we build highways? Where should we produce power? What areas should be preserved? Where should our parks, our wilderness areas, and our recreation facilities be?

We are told that in the next thirty years, 28,000 square miles of undeveloped land will be turned over for urban use and development. As a nation, we must strengthen the capacity of local communities and states to develop plans for our land use which anticipate these future needs rather than merely bringing the greatest return for the developer. Such plans may mean that developers will have to forego high profits in the interest of developing high quality environment.

Presently, developers are determining the destiny of our remaining resources without historical and cultural perspectives, and certainly without deeper spiritual values. It is crucial that these decisions be made on the basis of broader human values—values that relate to space, the room to wander, and to be stimulated by the Creation. Such decisions cannot be made purely on the basis of profit and loss. Far broader intangible values must be brought into account, and this can be done only by the input of those from many walks of life who have a concern for the whole person.

Let us consider the example of parks. In the past, we have usually decided to establish parks either for the purpose of preserving a national site or on the basis of various commercial and economic considerations. Now we must understand that parks, land, space, and beauty are qualities that are essential in preserving and nurturing the human spirit. The very process of creating parks must include considerations consistent with the purpose for their establishment. It is worth noting that the officials in Uganda never asked the IK people about moving away from their traditional hunting grounds. They never involved the IK people in their decision. An insensitive decision, albeit one concerned with preserving a natural resource, therefore, led to the destruction of the spirit of a people.

Although our values, and our need for spiritual vision, lie at the heart of the relentless forces threatening to despoil the earth, the solution involves more than merely raising our consciousness. Legislation is needed (and has in fact passed the Senate, but been frustrated in the House) that would purposely focus attention on the decision-making process over the use of our land. It would involve in the decision process the various levels of government, the people, the professionals, and all groups concerned with the issue. This is the kind of action required if we are to shape the course of our future rather than be victimized by competing economic forces not open to the need for input of deeper values.

Our external crowdedness is a paradigm of the inner condition of our lives. Obsessed with all we think we must do, we erode our capacity just to be.

Conceptual space is just as crucial as physical space. We need both the space and the time simply to think and to contemplate. On many days, I feel so totally frustrated, so involved with the details of each little routine in which I find myself that I will often rise up from the morass and indignantly proclaim, "When can I think?" This is a basic problem in all of our society. The inner space to reflect and contemplate is violated by the external stimuli that bombard the inhabitants of our electronic global village. The opportunity for thought, the capacity for silence, for meditation —these are as important qualities for modern humanity to preserve and to recapture as any I know. The spiritual void in which we find ourselves is nourished by the frantic pace of activity in modern society. We are running from ourselves, for we fear to be alone, and to be simply still.

Contemplation and the preservation of nature go hand in hand. Our tendency to abuse and ruin the created world mirrors our disregard for spiritual reality, both within ourselves and throughout the earth.

Many will ask, however, whether this concern for creation is just a luxury that can be afforded only by the affluent. It is said that the poor cannot afford the time to worry about ecology; that it is irrelevant to those who must worry about whether their children will be well fed, whether they will have any work, and whether they will be safe from violence.

I would reply that our concern is for the total environment in which we all are living. The poor in our inner cities are the chief victims of a society built with a distorted relationship to the land and to the whole of our environment. As we have allowed the process of massive urbanization to continue unabated, and as our cities have become increasingly "unlivable" for the affluent, we have consigned them to the poor. Even our "urban renewal" plans, in general, have either been plans to attract the middle class back into the city, displacing and uprooting the poor by increasing property values, or efforts to build low-income housing that all those who plan, design and execute would find intolerable to live in themselves. Yet we expect the poor to be happy there, and are bewildered by the general failure of such projects.

As the cities' parks become less safe and rivers and lakes become more polluted, any genuine sense of nature is possible only by retreating far from urbanization. The rich can bear the deterioration in the quality and livability of urban life, for they can always escape. The poor are not so fortunate.

Our concern, then, is not just for the preservation of untouched enclaves of nature's beauty—as important as that is—but for the totality of the relationship of all in society to their environment. And the relationships we build with our man-made communities and God-made world must be of the sort that can nurture the growth of the whole person. That will come only as "development" is freed from the dictates of economics, and made subservient to the demands of the human spirit.

Preserving the quality of life and community must begin, therefore, by accepting the concept of the common humanity of all, no longer thinking in terms of national borders or political ideology. We must consciously adopt values that transcend all these humanly established obstacles in order to overcome the threats universally confronting the total living environment for all the earth's citizens.

In less than thirty years, we must prepare the homes, schools, hospitals, factories, workshops, airports, roads, canals, leisure facilities and all the other buildings and structures to satisfy the requirements of a nearly doubled world population. We cannot make these decisions without examining our values and recognizing that today we are in a dead rush toward crisis, as we use and waste certain resources of humanity and nature which in many cases can never be replaced.

We have to recognize and remember the lessons from the IK. As we read at the conclusion of *The Mountain People*:

The IK teach us that our much vaunted human values are not inherent in humanity at all, but are associated only with a

particular form of survival called society, and that all, even
society itself, are luxuries that can be dispensed with. That
does not make them any the less wonderful or desirable and
if man has any greatness it is surely in his ability to maintain
these values, clinging to them to an often very bitter end, even
shortening our already pitifully short life rather than sacrificing
his humanity. But that too involves choice and the IK teach us
that man can lose the will to make it.[5]

If we take a quiet moment to think our future through—
to look on from the edge of history and recognize the possibilities that face us—I think our direction becomes clear.
To enhance our attachment to the transcendent is a spiritual
endeavor, requiring a sense of personal rebirth, and yielding
a dedication to the common humanity of us all. Unlike the
IK, we still have choices before us.

When I return to the stump overlooking the Oregon coast,
I discover a peacefulness of heart and a simplicity of spirit.
In the solitude of that special place, I am overwhelmed with
the urgency for the Body of Christ to nurture a clarity of
vision and a dedication to the values instilled by this kind
of communion with the creation.

If we are to allow God's Spirit to renew the face of the
earth, the Body of Christ must witness with peculiar clarity
and power to the truth that we are not the owners of
creation, but rather its stewards, entrusted with its temporary
use. We each must live and act in ways that demonstrate
loving stewardship of the whole of creation for all of humanity. In so doing, we must fashion those environments,
in our cities and in the country, which truly nurture the
whole person, and his or her relationship to creation. The
phrase describing followers of Christ as "salt of the earth"
today has greater material significance than we may realize.

Chapter 13

Bones
and Bounty

I WAS reading the Weekly Reader and I saw the boy on the front. You can see his bones. Would you buy the cattle from the farmers and give it to the poor?"

"The little boy was eating a little piece of bean and they should have more in their mouth, don't you think? I do. They are starving to death. If we was them they would send food to us. Why don't you do something?"

"I know of the money and the tax, but does money matter more than lives? I hope not."

These are the thoughts of grade school students from Yamhill, Oregon, who wrote me about world hunger. Their simple and pure human reactions to the needs of others throughout the world should be the starting point for any

197

truly mature reflection about the crisis of hunger and poverty in the world.

From the mid-'50s to the early '60s, the civil rights struggle was the dominant corporate moral concern in our nation. From the middle of that decade until 1975, the war in Indochina replaced that concern as the primary ethical crisis facing America. For the next ten years, I believe the deepest moral challenge we face is the injustice of a world dramatically split between the wealthy and the impoverished.

The most grave division in the world today is no longer between the East and the West; the division is not ideological. Rather, the division of the world which must concern us most for the future is economic: the division between the rich and the poor; the division between the North—the United States, Europe, Japan, and the Soviet Union, all the industrialized, developed powers in the world—and the South —the 49 nations of the world with a per capita gross national product of less than $275.

This is the poverty belt, the "Fourth World," where the truly wretched of the world's poor struggle for existence. How the rich nations relate to their poor neighbors will determine the prospects for true peace for us all in the decades ahead.

Hunger and starvation most vividly portray the realities of this division, and the suffering which is the result. What is the human effect of constant hunger and malnutrition? Listen to this picture:

> . . . the light of curiosity absent from children's eyes. Twelve-year-olds with the physical stature of eight-years-olds. Youngsters who lack the energy to brush aside the flies collecting about the sores on their faces. Agonizingly slow reflexes of adults crossing traffic. Thirty-year-old mothers who look sixty. All are common images in developing countries; all reflect inadequate nutrition, all have societal consequences.[1]

Multiply those word images by millions all across the globe and you begin to understand the incalculable human costs of insufficient food.

All that suffering can be summarized in cold statistics: 10,000 people starving every day; 426 million severely malnourished; untold numbers of children's bodies and minds permanently stunted by poor diets; more millions decimated by what ordinarily would be mild diseases.

The media have been jammed with the recitation of these facts and their graphic description, but hunger is still remote from us, for our stomachs are full.

Obviously, the effects of world food shortage do not fall equally on the rich and the poor. While the increase in food prices affects virtually everyone, it is not a matter of survival to citizens of rich nations. While people die for lack of a slice of bread, livestock in affluent nations consume vast quantities of grain to produce meat. The 370 million tons of grain used by rich countries to feed animals in 1969–1971 exceeded the total human consumption of cereal grains by the combined populations of China and India, which together comprise 30 percent of the world's population.[2] In 1975, higher grain prices slowed increases in animal grain consumption, and more cattle were being range-fed for longer periods, but the basic pattern has not been altered.

The food shortage may not appear to be as severe today as a year or two ago. At least it is no longer a constant news item in our headlines and on our television screens. There is every indication, however, that relief from outright famines is only temporary, and that the food shortage is not a passing aberration, but a long-term crisis of the gravest proportions.

In November of 1974, I was able to attend the United Nations World Food Conference in Rome. The documents prepared as a part of that conference portray the scope of the problem facing the world in the coming decade. If present trends continue, between 1970 and 1985 food demand in developed rich countries is expected to rise at an annual rate of 1.5 percent; that means a 26 percent increase in demand in that fifteen years. For the same period, food demand in the developing poor countries is projected at an annual growth rate of 3.6 percent, an increase in total food volume of about 70 percent between 1970 and 1985. To satisfy these increases in world demand, assuming present consumption

patterns, world agriculture from now until 1985 will have
to produce each year these additional amounts compared
to 1970 totals:

  230 million tons more of cereals for direct human con-
    sumption than in 1970
  nearly 40 million tons more of sugar
  110 million tons more of vegetables
  60 million tons more of meat
  140 million tons more of milk

By 1985, the world will have to be producing 520 million
tons more of primary cereal grains for all uses than in 1970,
an increase of 43 percent in fifteen years. The majority of
the increase in demands will come from the developing
countries.[3] In other words, if we do not change our basic
patterns of food consumption, the total amount of basic food
and grains required in the world to meet the projected demands of the market ten years from now will be almost half
again as much as the world was producing in 1970. And as a
tragic footnote, the experts point out what is seen as "demand" for food in the market may not at all be equal to the
amount actually needed in poorer countries for adequate
nutrition.

   Throughout most of the Fourth World, the internal demand for food caused by rising population far exceeds increases in food production. In Africa, for example, the
demand for cereal grains will increase by 76 percent between
1970 to 1985, while the increase in production will rise only
45 percent. What this means is that the poor nations will
need more and more food from outside their borders to feed
their people. The United Nations estimates that the developing nations will need between 15 to 20 million tons of grain
from the rich countries in order to meet their needs in 1976.
This they must obtain either through trade or as direct
foreign aid. But by 1985, that figure is projected to rise to
85 million tons. Only the most optimistic believe that the
rich nations could have such a surplus by then: even if they

did, the costs of transferring it as aid to the needy would require billions of dollars.

This picture becomes all the more tragic when we realize that the world has the capacity to produce food for all humanity's needs, both now and by 1985, if the consumption of food were more evenly and justly distributed throughout the globe.

Most traditional strategies of development and "foreign aid" overlook these realities, and concentrate on the following objectives:

1. An increase in support for rural development, with particular emphasis on productive investments in the agriculture and technical assistance for the farmer, especially sophisticated technology;
2. Reliance on the high-yield varieties of grain and the technologies needed to support their production, i.e., the Green Revolution;
3. Increasing attention to population, with the developed nations to impose zero population growth on the developing nations as a means of curbing demand;
4. The creation of a world food bank controlled by an international agency, and drawn upon in time of need as a defense against emergency situations created by natural disasters or war.

These proposals have formed the core of existing plans to deal with the world food crisis. Yet none of them offers anything really new; all are traditional concepts of the conventional wisdom which has failed to alter the gap between the rich and the poor. The fatal flaw is that all these propositions are paternalistic, or what some call culturally imperialistic. They seek to impose our wishes and our concepts, rooted in our particular history, on other cultures, societies, and economies that have entirely different dreams.

Most efforts at rural development in the past have been based on a "trickle down" theory of economics. Assistance is given to those farmers who are prosperous enough to utilize the technology of American methods of agriculture. The truly poor farmers and peasants remain unaffected. The same holds true for the "Green Revolution," which is a success only for those who can afford it.

It is imperative to remember that the principal cause of world hunger is poverty. No one starves who has money in his or her pocket. The principle cause of poverty, in turn, is unemployment.

At one point during the World Food Conference, the representative from Tanzania, next to whom I was sitting, said, "How foolish for some of these countries to be talking about capital intensive investment. In my country if we had a tractor there would be one man running the tractor and a thousand men watching him run the tractor. We need labor intensive development."

What directions must future global policies take, particularly if the poor nations are to enhance their own ability to become self-sufficient in food? Above all, it is hard to envision successful development in the poor nations if comprehensive land reform and income redistribution are not made the first tasks. This reform should be aimed at creating land units large enough to accommodate the single family living on them, and small enough that the land can be worked without substantial inputs of technology and energy required by American methods of agriculture. Needed heavy capital investments would be financed by cooperatives serving these small landholders rather than urban bureaucrats or foreign corporations. Outside assistance in the form of technical aid should all be directed toward facilitating the operation and production of these small units and their co-operative organizations, by-passing as much as possible profiteering bureaucrats and middlemen.

This emphasis on relatively small farms would accomplish several goals at once: (1) it would help stop the flight from rural areas to the even worse condition of urban slums by protecting the small farmer's land from acquisition by the rich elite; (2) rural development of this kind would foster rural employment by the maximum use of labor-intensive methods; (3) rural employment would begin to create for the rural poor the small measure of prosperity that so enhances population control efforts; (4) marketing procedures would be simplified and distribution costs reduced through the operation of cooperatives, to the benefit of rural producer and urban consumer alike.

There is no question about the obstacles which lie in this path. Chief among them are national elites in poor countries who resist such fundamental internal reforms because of the threat such steps pose to their own base of power. There is no assurance that the leaders of poor nations will naturally choose those policies most beneficial to the whole of their people. In such situations, the danger is that our external assistance, regardless of the motivations behind it, may only further solidify the power of such elites. Our aid then becomes a means of political manipulation rather than a tool of human development. What is required is the commitment that human liberation from need shall be the guiding priority of our policies of foreign aid and foreign trade, rather than the protection of our narrow political or economic interests. These proposals do not comprise a naive advocacy of idealism, but a realistic prescription of mandatory actions in order to feed humanity's children.

More realistically still, we must accept the fact that even the most optimistic hopes for agricultural development in the poor nations will not solve the long-term crisis of hunger unless global patterns of consumption and distribution are also transformed.

Each of us living in America consumes every year nearly a ton of cereal grains, the most basic food and form of protein. But only about 150 pounds of this is consumed directly in the form of bread, pastry, or breakfast cereals. The remaining 1850 pounds is consumed indirectly in the form of meats, milk and eggs.

By contrast, an average person living in a poor country has only about 400 pounds of cereal grains to consume each year for protein. This he or she must take directly as rice or bread from wheat, for little or none can be spared for more costly and inefficient means of protein production, as, for example, meat.

Because of our eating habits in the rich nations, it takes five times more of the limited resources of land, water, and fertilizer to support our diet than it would to support the diet of a Nigerian, or Colombian, or Indian, or Chinese. The amount of food and protein consumed by the diets of 210 million Americans could feed 1.5 billion Africans and Indians on a stable, though vastly different diet. On the whole, about two-thirds of the world's population fights for one-third of the world's total protein.

Our vast consumption of world energy resources is also related directly to the way we produce food. In a poor nation, or "primitive" culture, each calorie or unit of energy invested produces anywhere from 5 to 50 food calories. But in the rich nations it takes between 5 to 10 calories of energy to get just one food calorie.

Apply that to just one country such as India. If all of India's 550 million people were to be fed at our level of 3000 calories each day, it is estimated that it would require the expenditure of more energy than India currently uses for all other purposes. On a larger scale, to feed the entire world on our diet would require 80 percent of the world's total energy.

World hunger, then, exists not because of insufficient food, but because its distribution is determined by those who can pay the price. Hence, we may say that the food crisis "is caused by plunder, not by scarcity." [4]

I believe that part of the change required must involve the readjustment of our voracious lifestyles. The resources necessary to accomplish the elimination of poverty in the Fourth World will not be available if we continue to regard our planet as quarry for exploitation. Kenneth Boulding said years ago that anyone who believes man can forever go on plundering the resources of a finite earth must be either a madman or an economist.[5] Whatever the specific time frame, it is apparent now that the size of the pie is limited, and the amount we consume and the way in which we consume it are going to affect our ability to transfer the resources to the poor that will enable them to break free from the bondage of poverty. If we have a commitment to ending world hunger, then it is best that we begin this change now, before we come to regard a fixed, inequitable portion of the world's resources as intrinsically "ours."

The way we go about devising and implementing development policies must be grounded in an ethic that recognizes the essential oneness and commonality of humanity. The world's food and resources belong to all humanity and must be shared for the benefit of all. In so doing, we follow the wise words of Gandhi: "The earth provides enough for every man's need, but not enough for every man's greed."

This final change must come from within our hearts.

As Christians consider the issue of world impoverishment, we must recognize at the outset our clear mandate of love for all those who need. Our approach to world hunger must not be compromised by calculations of economic self-interest or political advantage. We have a direct and immediate responsibility to show forth by the shape of our own lives the love which our Lord exemplified. Then, but only then, when our lives are an authentic model of our convictions, we have the duty of judging and working for global policies on the basis of sacrificial love for all in need, as demonstrated by Christ.

One person I have encountered shows forth the concrete shape of this love perhaps more purely than anyone else I know. In March, 1974, I had the privilege not only to be in a place of intense suffering and famine—Calcutta—but also to spend a day in the presence of this person, a living saint of God, Mother Teresa of the Missionaries of Charity. My wife and I and our two oldest children, Elizabeth and Mark, followed Mother Teresa that day through the various parts of her ministry. She went to the lepers, reaching out and touching them as an expression of her personal love and concern. We visited the places where mothers brought their babies because they could no longer feed them. We saw Mother Teresa's ministry of picking up the dying elderly people from the streets, bathing them, feeding them, nursing them, loving them when others had left them to die alone.

She told us of an incredible incident of sharing which occurred when she took a portion of rice to the home of a needy family. The mother of the household reported that the five members of her family had not eaten for three days. As Mother Teresa portioned out the rice she noticed that the mother was picking up some of the rice and placing it into another vessel. Puzzled, she inquired for what it was to be used. The mother replied that there was a neighbor family which had not eaten for three days either. She wanted to share her rice with them. "I could have given a double portion of rice," Mother Teresa told us, "but I did not want to deny this family the blessing of sharing." I was struck by the profound truth acted out in that one simple incident. This needy mother realized that God had given her relative wealth and that she too had a responsibility to share it with those in need. She had learned through experience that it is more blessed to give than to receive.

We can glimpse this same quality in the life of Martin Niemöller, a German pastor imprisoned by the Nazis during World War II. It was in prison that he experienced what he called his "second conversion." Niemöller had so despised the atrocities of the Hitler regime that he came to hate the prison guard who brought him his food each day. Seeing the Nazi insignia on his uniform, all the indignation and outrage Niemöller felt toward that evil system was directed against that guard. Then, Niemöller tells us how one day he suddenly realized that Jesus Christ died, on the cross, for that guard; that Christ loved him that much. And in the same fashion, Niemöller was bound to love that guard, and love every person. The atonement of Christ took on a whole new meaning for Niemöller. Its implications were revolutionary, for every person was to be loved with the sacrificial love of Jesus Christ.

Under the cross of Christ, which Paul says is foolishness to the world but the power of God to those who are being saved, we can understand the scope of God's love. When we grasp this love in the depths of our being, then we will avoid separating the message of the Gospel from its mission.

One of the tragedies of the Church today is the unbiblical separation we have made between verbal witnessing to the Good News of Christ, and acting with his love to meet the needs of our fellow man. No such division exists in the Scriptures; none exists in the life of Christ. We do not find this split in the lives of saints like Mother Teresa, John Wesley, and so many others through the ages. We have created a false dichotomy, which we must allow God to destroy.

The message of God's redeeming love in Jesus Christ is inseparable from the living witness of that love, in each of our lives, for others. There are two great commandments, which together make the whole Gospel—to love God with all our heart, soul, strength and mind, and to love our neighbor as ourselves. "If you heed my commandments, you will dwell in my love," our Lord said (John 15:10). If our lives have been truly touched by the miraculous, redeeming love of Christ, and if we are dwelling in that love, then we wil be living forth the wholeness of the Gospel. Our lives will be a natural witness, in all that we do and say, to Christ's love for every person.

Martin Niemöller suddenly realized that day that his Nazi prison guard, with all of the hatred and brokenness in his life, stood beneath the shadow of the cross. He was loved by God as is every person.

To nurture in the center of our being the indwelling love of Christ leads us to love all whom he loves, both in intimately personal relationships and with an overall corporate sense of his love. In our one-to-one relationships, we must discover ever anew the miracle of that love which pours itself out, purely for the sake of the other, with abandon to the self. This is the love which strives to see each individual as God does—as a person with the potential to be fully free, whole and redeemed, through the power of Christ; to envision each person with that same quality of love which led Christ from Gethsemane to Golgotha. In marriage, with our families, with those in our churches, and with those where we work, this is how we must strive to love and relate in our daily, face-to-face relationships.

But our love must not stop there. For Christ calls us into a love that knows no boundaries, no limitations, other than the scope of human need. Throughout the Old and New Testament, we read again and again about God's focused

compassion for those who suffer, who are poor, who are
hungry, who are oppressed, and who are in need.

"Who is our neighbor," our Lord was asked. In response
he related the story of the Good Samaritan. Our neighbor
was not simply the person next door, or our circle of close
friends. He was anyone downtrodden, distraught, and victimized by the world's pain and inhumanity—anyone whom
we encounter at his or her point of need.

As our lives begin to touch the reality of this love, which
flows only as God's gift, we discover a love that extends to
all humanity. The closer we are to the cross, the more keenly
we feel the pain and suffering of humanity everywhere.

Christ is the Bread of Life. It is he who gives us our own
life, spiritually and physically. But if a person spends his
waking hours struggling for enough physical bread to avoid
starvation, there is little chance of his hearing the spiritual
message. How can we possibly share the message of Christ,
the Bread of Life, to such a person without trying to fill his
or her empty stomach with food?

When Christ began his public ministry the first words he
uttered, as we have already noted in chapter 4, were a reading from the book of Isaiah. "He has anointed me to preach
the good news to the poor; he has sent me to heal the broken-
hearted, to proclaim release to the captives and recovering
of sight to the blind; to set at liberty those who are oppressed;
to proclaim the acceptable year of the Lord" (Luke 4:18–19,
RSV). Both the Old and the New Testaments admonish us to
feed even our enemies when they are hungry (Prov. 25:21;
Rom. 12:20).

Faced with these realities, and filled with the compassion
of Christ, what is our response? Above all, we must allow
our hearts to be made sensitive to the suffering of fellow
humanity. The facts and statistics must be translated into
human realities which we can feel from deep within, and
which will quicken our conscience.

We should allow ourselves to feel uncomfortable about
our wealth, our life-style, our diet, and all our subtle worship
of affluence. We must let God's spirit move within us, even

to convict us anew of sin, and to show us the ways of repentance and renewal. Most of all, let us cast aside all those rationalizations that would somehow prevent us from understanding and reaching out to those who suffer.

There are some who write, or seem to say, that perhaps all the worst about famine, disaster, and war will indeed come true, and that this only indicates and prepares us for the Second Coming of Christ. Without embarking on a lengthy eschatological discussion, we can agree about one central biblical truth. We are never told to sit by and watch the world destroy itself in its inhumanity and sin, and console ourselves with the prediction that the end of all things must be just around the corner. To turn our back on the suffering of the world is to turn away from Christ himself. This is exactly what he has told us.

> "When the Son of Man comes in his glory and all the angels with him, he will sit in state on his throne, with all the nations gathered before him. He will separate men into two groups, as a shepherd separates sheep from the goats. . . . Then the king will say to those on his right hand, 'You have my Father's blessing; come, enter and possess the kingdom that has been ready for you since the world was made. For when I was hungry, you gave me food; when thirsty, you gave me drink. . . . I tell you this: anything you did for one of my brothers here, however humble, you did for me" (Matt. 25:31–40).

It is precisely because all history is consummated in him—because Christ is Lord over all—that we must give our lives in his service to the world's need. In so doing, we are proclaiming and giving witness to his love and his victory.

I have no patience for those who say that people are poor or suffering because it is "God's will" and thus there is nothing we should do for them. It is God's will that "every valley shall be exalted; every hill made low; the crooked made straight, and the rough places plain" (Isa. 40:4). God's will was proclaimed in Mary's words when the angel announced that she would give birth to Christ: "The hungry

he has satisfied with good things; the rich sent empty away"
(Luke 1:53).

Thomas Merton has written:

> It is easy enough to tell the poor to accept their poverty as
> God's will when you yourself have warm clothes and plenty
> of food and medical care and a roof over your head and no
> worry about the rent. But if you want them to believe—try
> to share some of their poverty and see if you can accept it as
> God's will yourself![6]

The command and compassion of Christ compels us to
respond to the physical and spiritual needs of a hungry
world.

What concretely can we do?

I think often our first inclination as Christians is to look
to government. But this is not always the answer. Often, in
fact, that amounts to asking Caesar to undertake what is
basically a spiritual ministry. What may seem to be a purely
material act can in reality require an undergirding spiritual
response. Government is limited by its priorities in a way
which the Christian church is not. The greatest commandment we have is to love God and to love our neighbors. And
love is not an emotion. It is action.

We must ask ourselves some very basic questions. What
does it mean to be the salt of the earth? What does it mean
to be crucified with Christ, to deny ourselves and to take up
the cross daily? The time is ripe for Christians to act individually and corporately in a manner consistent with being
crucified with Christ, with the denial of ourselves, with true
separation from the world—a separation not defined by
legalism but by the way in which we respond to the world's
hurt and pain. We must avoid being squeezed into the world's
mold.

As we each approach holiday seasons we should ask ourselves how we can make the celebration of these special times
different from the manner in which they are normally cele-
brated. Why holidays? Simply because on holidays we usually
overeat! Indeed, we should adopt a changed consumption
pattern for all days. For centuries Christians have approached

special seasons by fasting. Pope Leo I in the fifth century said, "What we forego by fasting is to be given as alms to the poor." [7]

Of course we can give to the agencies of humanitarian outreach who are committed to alleviating the world's suffering. But we are far beyond the point of thinking that a few dollars given once a year will be sufficient to fulfill our responsibility. Our talents and skills are called for. We can give them, voluntarily, to this mission, and even take a year or two to go ourselves, and help serve those in need.

But even while we are aware of the world-wide hunger, it is easy, and convenient, to forget the hunger and suffering in our own home town. And make no mistake—it is there. We have poor and oppressed, suffering the effects of hunger and malnutrition, throughout our own land, living side by side with our society's affluence and abundance. In each of our cities, the gifts and potential of countless individuals are maimed in the earlier years of life because of a lack of food, particularly protein. That is corporate sin in the eyes of God. So if we are touched by Christ's Spirit for those who are suffering and hungry, then let us begin with our neighbor here at home.

But then, let us allow that compassion to flow in its fullness for all who suffer everywhere, for they all are our neighbors.

Let me offer some specific suggestions:
—Every congregation could establish a specific budget amount directed to meeting the needs of starving people in some particular point of the world.
—Christians could be asked to give a specific tithe just for the purpose of relieving hunger; further we could consider a graduated tithe, which increases in its percentage according to the amount of one's income. "From those to whom much has been given, much will be expected."
—We should renew the Christian discipline of fasting as a means for teaching us how to identify with those who hunger, and to deepen our life of prayer for those who suffer.

—We must all analyze, in prayer before God, our own habits of food consumption. Specifically, we can drastically alter our consumption of meat, and the money we save we can give to alleviate world hunger.

—Finally, we must prayerfully examine our overall standard of material wealth in light of the world's need.

What is our life-style? Is it characterized by consumption or by conservation? What determines our needs—the television, friends, culture? What determines our buying patterns today? More gadgets—the best, the most colorful, the easiest to care for, the throw-aways with their convenience and disposability?

In addition to our individual involvement as members, the Church can act corporately. Let us recall that the Church of Jesus Christ was the reforming influence of the eighteenth and nineteenth centuries: putting an end to child labor, abolishing slavery, caring for the needy. We should not totally abdicate this work to agencies which do not have the underpinning of love and motivation of Jesus Christ. The churches, as Christian communities, can act, and not merely adopt statements and resolutions.

We can adopt a needy family just as we support missionaries. We can help that family to reenter the world of employment.

We can decry wasteful eating habits, setting the example of change in life-style, and again encourage the money saved to be spent on humanitarian efforts. One church in Texas has reduced the cost of a building expansion program by one-third, giving that third to hunger relief.

We can form food cooperatives which can fundamentally change the ways in which we buy our food, so that we support the small farmer rather than the large corporation.

These are only suggestions. But the point is that Christ's love beckons us to far more than simply charitable giving. He calls us to love, and to give in a way that changes the shape of our lives. His love for us led him to the cross. And it will lead us, if we follow, to pour ourselves out for the sake of others. This is how the world can come to know

Christ as Lord. We may be led in many different ways in the course of our individual calling and service. Our common task is to open ourselves to the promptings of the Spirit, and then follow, giving forth this sacrificial love to the needs of others.

If we really believe that God loved us while we were yet sinners, then we will not wait for the poor and the outcasts of society to earn the right to be loved in our eyes. Nor will we demand that they show due appreciation for what we are doing for them. We will avoid all the lame excuses that prejudice us against the poor, the needy, the dispossessed. We will love them because of the cross, because we have been shown in our own lives that people do not need to deserve love or to earn love.

Our responsibility as Christians is to call the nation to a rightful exercise of stewardship. The Bible makes it clear that a people will be judged on how they utilize the gifts given to them. We will be judged, then, on what we do with the abundance and wealth which is ours. As a nation, we have the duty of stewardship over all our material, natural, and human resources; they can be used for life or for death, for our own selfish and wasteful consumption, or for the benefit of all humanity. We must apply these perspectives to the secular political realms of decision-making.

What is love of country, if not pleading with a nation to choose the priorities of life? Is it not true concern for the spirit of a people which calls them forth to the service of human need?

We must be prepared to hear God's word of judgment upon our nation, for hope comes only when we acknowledge our fallenness and repent. But then, we must also offer a word, and an example, of hope and renewal.

What is our country, if not our land and our bountiful resources of all kinds, and above all, the people? So let us love the land, and preserve it as an environment which nurtures the whole life of our people. Let us be stewards of justice over our resources, sharing and utilizing them for the sake of all humanity. And let all of us be inspired to a relevant and sacrificial commitment of our lives to the destiny of those who are poor, hungry, and oppressed. Then shall we discover true greatness, even that shown to us by the One who came to serve, and emptied himself, washing the feet of others.

Epilogue

IT WAS A brisk autumn day in late 1975. In the morning I went down to the Senators' Dining Room in the Capitol with two close members of my staff. Over coffee, they explained to me that there were legal technicalities which would prohibit me, as a Senator, from directly assisting, in a way I earnestly desired, the social mission of a particular Christian organization. On that day this suddenly seemed like the last straw.

"Maybe I'm just going to have to get out of this life," I quietly said. They knew I was talking seriously. One of them had heard the same words at the airport five years earlier. Now they sat in stunned silence, struggling for some response.

We talked more, and I shared some of the frustrations I was feeling over the demands of successful political life and the tensions produced with the other values to which I yearn

215

216 Between a Rock and a Hard Place

to give myself. I was pressured, it seemed, from nearly every side. Love for my wife and four children beckoned me to forget all else in order to give myself more fully to them. The simple financial burden of being in politics, having no other private wealth, and of necessity maintaining residences in Washington, D.C., and Oregon, seemed overpowering. Life in the U.S. Senate appeared best suited for only the independently rich. The necessity of trips back to Oregon to maintain ties with my constituents often conflicted with the urgent legislative tasks I was pursuing in the Senate; together, these priorities ruled out accepting most all invitations from Christian groups, schools, and churches who were asking me to visit. That intensified my frustration, for I longed to take part in various means of ministry and outreach with other Christians.

Walking back to my office, I said, "Maybe I just try too much to be a 'Purist.' Perhaps I should forget about that all, and play the game just like most everyone else. That would make things a lot easier."

It took a few hours for my frustration of that morning to subside, and for my mood to change as I recovered a deeper perspective on these issues. As I did, it helped focus my attention once again on the basic vision and values to which I have committed my life. I knew I had to persevere.

The central issue is whether I believe that the shape of God in Jesus Christ, taking human form in history, is politically axiomatic for me today. Am I truly to stake my life on the conviction that the character of life and quality of love I see in Christ is to be reproduced in me, fundamentally shaping the style of my political activity?

Christ emptied himself. He took on the form of a servant. Though rich, Paul tells us, for our sake he became poor. He was counted among the outcast. He forsook the temptations of earthly power out of fidelity to the Kingdom he came to establish. He gave of himself to deliver the poor and the oppressed out of their bondage. He prayed that not his will, but God's be done. He delivered himself into the hands of sinful men, rather than retaliate to their evil.

He loved without conditions. He spoke God's prophetic truth without fear. And he was crucified as a common criminal, dying so that we might have Life.

He proclaimed the emergence of God's Kingdom—the rule of true justice and righteousness. He called those who followed him to build that Kingdom by living as a new community of God's people. To those who followed him, he said that the first shall be last, and the last first; that we must lose our lives in order to find them; and that greatness consists of the most humble acts of servanthood.

If we are called to Christ, then our lives are to take on his own shape. Whether teachers, doctors, businessmen, politicians, lawyers, laborers, or ministers, our first task is to embody the quality of Christ's life. Faithfulness to this call totally transcends any requirements of "success" posed by our vocations or the conformist opinions of society.

Identified truly with Christ, we will find ourselves serving the oppressed of the world—the victims of injustice and sin. We will begin to look at the structures of society from the vantage point of the poor.

Our hope rests in the promise of God's ongoing love, and his intention to effect a new order in human affairs. This we first grasp among the people called to be the Body of Christ. There we discover God's revolutionary act of pouring his life into others, who share in common God's Spirit. We see the hope all things being renewed as this corporate life is given in sacrificial service for the world.

Our call is to faithfulness, not to efficacy; it is to servanthood rather than power. We know that the most decisive action that we can take to shape history is to follow the way of Christ, to give ourselves to the building of the Body, and to pour out ourselves as he did in love.

When Christ calls us, he calls us to join in building a new peoplehood, who are to be the world's salt and light. By the building of this community we become part of an authentic witness which demonstrates the shape of God's new order in the midst of a fallen world. From this point flow our mission, outreach, and hope; they rest not upon the world's

218   Between a Rock and a Hard Place

systems, but on the promise and presence of Christ and his Kingdom.

There is an old Jewish proverb which I recalled on that day last fall, and it continues to give me strength:

"God gives you the task. He does not ask that you succeed, but he does ask that you not lay it aside."

Notes

Chapter 3

1. From the minutes of the Young Life executive board meeting, August 1971. When the full board of directors met in December of that year, it adopted as official policy a position on civil disobedience that was based on Dr. Jewett's position paper. This was a most remarkable step for an evangelical organization, and one that I found most encouraging.
2. James Muilenburg, *The Way of Israel* (New York: Harper and Brothers, 1961). See pp. 74–98, "The Way of the Prophets." This is a good summary of the prophets' role in the Old Testament and their relationship to the governing authorities. I have found this source quite helpful in summarizing the message of the prophets in the five areas identified by Muilenburg.
3. John Bright, *The Kingdom of God* (New York: Abingdon-Cokesbury Press, 1953), p. 116. John Bright's excellent study of the Old Testament has a very fine summary of Jeremiah's message.
4. Jeremiah 12:7–8, cited in Bright, p. 117.

Chapter 4

1. See, for example, Oscar Cullman, *The State in the New Testament* (New York: Scribner's, 1956), p. 8 ff., for an excellent discussion of Jesus' relationship to the Zealots and the political climate of that day, which has been illuminating for me.
2. The most insightful discussion of the New Testament understanding of the "powers" which I have found is Hendrik Berkhof, *Christ and the Powers* (Scottdale, Pa.: Herald Press,

1962). I have relied heavily on his interpretation and work in the following pages dealing with this subject. John Howard Yoder's *Politics of Jesus* (Grand Rapids: Eerdmans, 1972), also utilizes Berkhof's interpretation in the chapter "Christ and Power," pp. 135–62.

Chapter 5

1. Berkhof, p. 25.
2. Ibid., p. 30.
3. Ibid., p. 15.
4. Ibid., pp. 25–26.
5. Ibid., p. 30.
6. Ibid., pp. 30–31.
7. Yoder, pp. 200–204, includes a helpful discussion of these distinctions.
8. C. E. B. Cranfield, "The Christian's Political Responsibility According to the New Testament," *Scottish Journal of Theology* XV, 1962, pp. 182–83, as quoted in Robert Sabath, "Paul's View of the State, Part One," *Post American*, April 1974, p. 9.
9. Sabath, ibid., p. 8. Part Two of this excellent article appeared in the May 1974 issue. I found the full manuscript by Robert Sabath with his 53 extensive (and unpublished) footnotes to be an excellent treatment of this subject.
10. F. F. Bruce, *The Book of Acts* (Grand Rapids: Eerdmans, 1971), p. 345, cited in Sabath, ibid., p. 10.
11. John Howard Yoder, *Christian Witness to the State* (Newton, Kan.: Faith and Life Press, 1964), p. 77. I first found this quote in an unpublished paper written by David Bennett, a student at Fuller Theological Seminary, "God, State, and War."

Chapter 6

1. G. J. Heering, *The Fall of Christianity* (New York: 1928), p. 24.
2. Cecil J. Cadoux, *The Early Church and the World* (Edinburgh: T. & T. Clark, 1925), pp. 249–50.
3. Ibid., p. 248.
4. Ibid.
5. Ibid., pp. 256–57.
6. Ibid., p. 360.

7. Ibid., p. 249.
8. J. C. Wenger, *Pacifism and Biblical Nonresistance* (Scottdale, Pa.: Herald Press, 1968), p. 10.
9. Cadoux, p. 272.
10. Ibid., p. 275.
11. Wenger, p. 8.
12. Roland H. Bainton, *Christian Attitudes toward War and Peace* (Nashville and New York: Abingdon, 1960), pp. 75–76.
13. Ibid., p. 77.
14. Cadoux, pp. 252–53.
15. Erwin Ramsdell Goodenough, *The Church in the Roman Empire* (New York: 1931), pp. 52–53.
16. Ibid., p. 43.
17. Adolph Harnack, *Militia Christi* (Tübingen: 1905), p. 92.
18. Ibid.
19. Cadoux, pp. 589–90.
20. Richard McSorely, *Kill for Peace?* (New York: Corpus Papers, 1970), p. 31.
21. Augustine, *Epistle to Marcellinus* (in Heering, *The Fall of Christianity*, pp. 59–60).

Chapter 8

1. Such examples are also elaborated on in Yoder's *Politics of Jesus,* chapter 4, "God Will Fight for Us," pp. 78–89. I first came across this view, however, in the paper by David Bennett (see n. 11, chap. 5).
2. This point is made in Bennett's paper previously referred to, which I have found illuminating for this discussion.
3. Zechariah's prophecy concerning Christ in Luke 1:79, which echoes the Psalmist's prophecy in Psalm 85:13.

Chapter 9

1. Thomas Merton, "Blessed Are the Peacemakers," pamphlet published by the Fellowship of Reconciliation (Box 271, New York, NY) in July 1967; reprinted from *Fellowship Magazine,* May 1967.
2. Quoted in John Howard Yoder, *Nevertheless* (Scottdale, Pa.: Herald Press, 1971), p. 32.
3. Gene Sharp, *The Politics of Nonviolent Action* (Boston: Porter Sargent, 1974).
4. *Niles Weekly Register* (Baltimore), Vol. II, No. 2, March 7,

1818, pp. 17–18. This is part of a lengthy letter written on February 13, 1818, to Mrs. Niles, printed in his *Weekly Register.* In another letter written from John Adams to Thomas Jefferson (in *The Adams-Jefferson Letters,* p. 455), Adams tells Jefferson, "As to the history of the Revolution, my Ideas may be peculiar, perhaps singular. What do We mean by the Revolution? The War? That was no part of the Revolution. It was only an Effect and Consequence of it. The Revolution was in the Minds of the People, and this was effected, from 1760 to 1775, in the course of fifteen Years before a drop of blood was drawn at Lexington."

5. These are summarized in an unpublished manuscript by Gene Sharp, "A New Defense Option?" (1974); also, they are explored along with numerous other cases in Sharp, *The Politics of Nonviolent Action.*

6. Gene Sharp, *The Politics of Nonviolent Action,* p. 4.

7. From *German Rule in Russia, 1941–1945* (London: Macmillan and Co., 1957), p. 498, as in Gene Sharp, "Control of Political Power and Conduct of Open Struggle," quoted in *American Defense Policy,* Mark E. Smith II and Claude J. Johns, Jr., eds. (Baltimore: Johns Hopkins Press), 2d ed., p. 530.

8. M. K. Gandhi, *Non-violence in Peace and War* (Ahmedabad, India: Navajivan Publishing House, 1948), Vol. I, p. 147, as quoted in *American Defense Policy,* p. 530.

9. Gene Sharp, "Defense Without War?," unpublished manuscript (1974), pp. 3–4.

10. Arthur F. Holmes, "War and Christian Ethics," *Reformed Journal,* February 1974, p. 20. In a two-part series appearing in the January and February 1974 issues of the *Reformed Journal,* Holmes cogently outlines Christian thinking on the subject of war, giving a summary of "pacifist" positions in Part One, and "just war" positions in Part Two, without committing himself specifically to either. I spoke at Wheaton College in February 1974 and then met Professor Holmes at a meeting with faculty members where the question of Christian thinking about violence was discussed. Professor Holmes then sent me these articles, from which I drew in presenting my own summary, particularly of just-war theory.

11. Edgar Jones, "One War Is Enough," *Atlantic Monthly,* February 1956, pp. 48–53.

12. Holmes, "War and Christian Ethics," *Reformed Journal,* February 1974, p. 20.
13. Ibid.

Chapter 10

1. John Hersey, *Hiroshima* (New York: Knopf, 1946).
2. William Thompson, *At the Edge of History* (New York: Harper & Row, 1971), p. 163.
3. Friedrich Nietzsche, *Schopenhauer As Educator* (Chicago: Gateway Editions, 1965), p. 37.
4. T. S. Eliot, "Choruses from the Rock," III, 4, in *The Complete Poems and Plays* (New York: Harcourt, Brace & Co., 1963), p. 103.
5. Fyodor Dostoyevsky, *The Brothers Karamazov* (New York: Signet Classics, 1957), p. 226.
6. E. F. Schumacher, *Small Is Beautiful* (New York: Harper & Row, 1973), p. 21.
7. Lewis Mumford, *The Pentagon of Power* (New York: Harcourt Brace Jovanovich, Inc., 1964), p. 413.
8. Archibald MacLeish, *New York Times* article, December 25, 1968, p. 1.
9. Schumacher, p. 31.
10. Thomas Merton, *New Seeds of Contemplation* (New York: New Directions, 1961), p. 122.

Chapter 11

1. E. F. Schumacher, *Small Is Beautiful* (New York: Harper & Row, 1973), p. 66.
2. Erich Fromm, *The Sane Society* (New York: Fawcett World Library, 1955), p. 312.
3. Leo Tolstoy, *Tolstois Flucht und Tod,* ed. Fülöp-Miller and F. Eckstein (Berlin: 1925), p. 103; translated and cited by Fromm, ibid., p. 188.

Chapter 12

1. See Frank Sartwell, "The Small Satanic Worlds of John Calhoun," *Smithsonian Magazine,* April 1970, p. 68 ff. Also, see John B. Calhoun, "The Lemmings' Periodic Journeys Are Not

Unique," *Smithsonian Magazine,* January 1971, especially p. 11.

2. Colin M. Turnbull, *The Mountain People* (New York: Simon & Schuster, 1972). Also, it is interesting to note that John B. Calhoun wrote about the IK and Turnbull's book, making comparisons with his own study of mice: John B. Calhoun, "Plight of the IK and the Kaiadilt Is Seen As a Chilling Possible End for Man," *Smithsonian Magazine,* November 1972, p. 27 ff.

3. "Pursuit of Happiness," *U.S. News and World Report,* August 27, 1973, p. 35.

4. Ibid., pp. 39–40.

5. Turnbull, p. 294.

Chapter 13

1. Alan Berg, *The Nutrition Factor* (Washington: The Brookings Institution, 1973), p. 9.

2. *World Hunger: Causes and Remedies,* A Transnational Institute Report, Washington and Amsterdam, October 1974. This report was issued in unpublished form shortly before the World Food Conference of that year. Its analysis is most thorough and helpful.

3. Ibid. The same figures appear in the documents prepared by the United Nations for the World Food Conference.

4. Ibid., p. 64.

5. Cited in Mancur Olson, "Introduction," *Daedalus,* Vol. 102, No. 4 (Fall 1974), p. 3. This is a special issue dealing with the limits-to-growth debate.

6. Thomas Merton, *New Seeds of Contemplation,* p. 179.

7. F. X. Weisner, *Handbook of Christian Feasts and Customs* (New York: Harcourt, Brace and World, 1958), p. 171.